A Proven Plan
for Beginning
New Habits

21 Days to *Financial* Freedom

Dan Benson

Series Editor
Dan Benson

ZondervanPublishingHouse
Grand Rapids, Michigan

A Division of HarperCollinsPublishers

21 Days to Financial Freedom
Copyright © 1998 by Dan Benson

Requests for information should be addressed to:

ZondervanPublishingHouse
Grand Rapids, Michigan 49530

ISBN: 0-310-21751-2

This book is intended to provide general information in regard to the subject matter covered. Neither the author nor the publisher is engaged in rendering legal, tax, investment, accounting, or other professional financial advice or services. Because every reader's financial situation and goals are unique and because financial products, market conditions, and laws or interpretations of laws are subject to change, it is recommended that a financial professional be consulted prior to implementing any of the suggestions herein.

Published in association with the literary agency of Alive Communications, Inc., 1465 Kelly Johnson Blvd. #320, Colorado Springs, CO 80920.

Interior design by Sherri L. Hoffman

Printed in the United States of America

98 99 00 01 02 03 04 /❖ DC/ 10 9 8 7 6 5 4 3 2 1

CONTENTS

PREFACE

21 Days to Financial Freedom

You probably have some good reasons for obtaining this book. You may be among the millions who stagger erratically from paycheck to paycheck. Perhaps you're struggling with consumer debt that makes you feel you'll never get ahead. Or maybe you've just had that discomforting feeling that you could be doing better than you are—that you need to achieve better control of your cash flow, put more away in savings, and even invest for future needs and dreams.

During the next 21 days, one step at a time, you're going to regain control of your financial life.

Why 21 days?

It's simple, really.

When you get right down to it, most personal financial problems are rooted in bad habits. Bad spending habits. Bad saving habits. Bad investing habits. Human performance specialists tell us that it takes 21 days to rid yourself of a bad habit and replace it with a new one. If you've been Mr. Couch Potato and decide to give aerobic exercise a try, it will take a thoughtful, consistent effort on your part for three straight weeks before your new regimen becomes a healthy habit. But the good news is, it takes only three weeks! If you hang in there for those 21 days, each day building on the progress and momentum of the preceding days, that exercise will become a natural part of your life. Indeed, if you skip a day, you will actually miss it.

Studies have shown the same to be true with practically any area of life in which you might desire a positive change: from overeater to careful eater; from smoker to nonsmoker; from spendthrift to saver; from Elephant Man to Tom Cruise. (Okay, so I exaggerate. But you get the idea.).

This simple, powerful principle is the foundation for the entire 21 Day series, and for this book, *21 Days to Financial Freedom*. As a former financial planner, I've worked with people just like you and rejoiced with them as they took the proper steps to turn their finances around. In their eyes I could see the transformation from frustration and anxiety to joy and peace of mind. I want the same for you!

STRATEGIES FOR FINANCIAL SUCCESS

During our 21-day journey together, you will learn how to

- gain control of your monthly cash flow;
- give yourself a raise, no matter what your boss says;
- get out of debt—and stay debt-free;
- discover thousands of dollars you didn't know you had;
- give more to your church, favorite ministry, or people in need;
- have the money you need, when you need it—for your next emergency, next vacation, next big purchase;
- save thousands on your next car;
- save thousands on life and auto insurance;
- save hundreds on next year's tax bill;
- know what kinds of insurance you need and what kinds to avoid like the plague;
- ensure a financially secure retirement.

FINANCIAL FREEDOM

What we're talking about here is *financial freedom*—freedom from debt, from too much month at the end of the money, from anxiety over your financial future. Financial freedom means knowing your bases are covered, that you're no longer pouring good cash down the drain of poor decisions, that you can finance a debt-free vacation or launch your own business venture, that you're building a healthy nest egg for your future.

So our purpose is to help you succeed with your money and enjoy peace of mind. Each day's lesson is brief, simple, to the point. Study each day and take the step or steps recommended for that day. It's as easy as that.

Within just a few days, you'll begin to notice a change. You'll feel you're starting to get your financial act together. As you progress along our 21-day journey, you'll find yourself breaking free from the harmful ways of your past and implementing sound strategies for your future. At the end of the 21 days, you'll have most of the essentials in place—and a set of healthy new habits.

I want to acknowledge and thank Dennis Means, CFP (Denver, Colorado), for reviewing the manuscript and giving valuable suggestions. Also, I thank my agent, Greg Johnson of Alive Communications, who believed in this project from its infancy and encouraged its first steps into the real world.

Before we start, you may want to get a pen and some paper. Go ahead, I'll wait. Use the pen to underscore insights and ideas that stand out to you. You'll also be doing some small but important pen-to-paper projects as we go. But don't worry: We'll keep it simple. We may even have some fun along the way.

Ready for financial freedom? Turn the page and let's begin.

DAN BENSON

FORT COLLINS, COLORADO

DAY 1

"If Only I Made More Money . . ."

Why "more money" is rarely the answer

Do you ever catch yourself thinking, *If only I made more money, then I could* . . . followed by a list of things that would be better?

Like: *Then I could save and invest more . . . then I could get outta debt . . . get a more reliable car . . . and afford a better home . . . and be ready when retirement comes. THEN I wouldn't worry so much about my finances.*

If you've entertained such thoughts, I'd like you to meet Jeff and MaryAnn.

They were typical of the couples I worked with as senior planner for a Denver financial planning firm. Upper thirties, above-average income, no devastating setbacks. Yet, financially, they were barely keeping their heads above water.

"It seems like we should have more to show for all our hard work," Jeff said during our initial meeting. "But as you can see, our monthly expenses consume just about everything."

"We'd really like to be putting some aside for retirement and for the kids' college education," MaryAnn joined in. "Really, we just need some breathing room. But with all our monthly expenses and then our insurance costs and Christmas and birthdays, there just isn't enough. If only we made more money . . ."

If only. Jeff and MaryAnn were stuck on a paycheck-to-paycheck treadmill. Their consumer debt demanded inordinate chunks of each month's available cash, and the budgetary pressures didn't seem to want to go away. Because they were so preoccupied with present obligations, their future financial goals were only wishful thinking.

Like Jeff and MaryAnn, all of us want to succeed with our money. And, since most of our parents didn't name us Bill Gates (my mom and dad decided to call me Dan, since that was my name), money pressures seem inevitable. Adlai Stevenson summed it up: "There was a time when a fool and his money were soon parted, but now it happens to everybody."

WHY MONEY PROBLEMS?

Financial pressures are not just a problem of low income. In 1960 a still-famous book titled *The Law and the Profits* swept management circles around the world. The author is C. Northcote Parkinson, whose parents realized too late that maybe they should have named *him* Bill, because the kids on the playground were ruthless about "Northcote." But Parkinson grew up to show up his playmates by thinking up the now-famous Parkinson's Law:

Work expands to fill the time available.

Parkinson's Law continues to be revered among businesspeople to this day, probably out of gratitude that it isn't called Northcote's Law. *Work expands to fill the time available* underscores a universal truth that workers had always suspected but were embarrassed to verbalize: that no matter how much time you're able to save in the workplace, your workload will always increase to fill the time you thought you had saved. It didn't embarrass Parkinson to say it because this was nothing compared to being called Northcote.

What many people don't remember is that within the same book, Parkinson made a second statement that in my view is even more prophetic than the first: *Expenditures rise to meet income.* Anyone who has ever managed a personal budget knows just how true, and embarrassing, this is.

Expenditures rise to meet income. Have you, like millions of others, ever promised yourself, "After my next raise, I'm going to get out of debt and save more"—only to see your personal expenses rise to equal or surpass the amount of the raise? And have you, like millions of others, promised yourself that if you can just get your debts paid off, you'll never go that deeply in debt again—only to see your debt balance soar to even loftier heights?

Once again, Parkinson nailed the probable reason: *Individual expenditure not only rises to meet income but tends to surpass it, and probably always will.* This was Jeff and MaryAnn's dilemma. Despite their good intentions and above-average income, their haphazard spending patterns had conformed to Parkinson's second law and placed them in financial bondage. Now they felt immobilized—unable to get out of debt and build for their future.

And Jeff and MaryAnn are not alone. In fact, theirs is the financial road most traveled in our world—the path of too-easy credit, of instant gratification, of "spend-it-while-we-got-it-and-even-if-we-don't" thinking. The path of least resistance had become a slippery slope of financial despair. And instead of backing up and choosing a surer path, they hoped for a quicker fix called "If only I made more money . . ."

YOU MAY ALREADY BE A MILLIONAIRE ...

Have you ever stopped to think how much money will go through your hands in a lifetime? If you average just $25,000 income per year between ages 25 and 65, you will have earned a total of *$1,000,000* by age 65. If you're now 35 and average $35,000 per year, you will earn $1,050,000 in the next thirty years. If you're 45 and averaging $50,000 per year, you will earn $1,000,000 over the next twenty years. Thus, for above-average earners like Jeff and MaryAnn, "more money" is not really the answer to financial problems. Without wiser stewardship, more money will only result in higher taxes, spending, and debt. Expenditures rise to meet income.

Fortunately, Jeff and MaryAnn typify only one financial path. I've also worked with individuals and couples with similar (sometimes smaller) incomes, but who had been able to build a small fortune in savings and investments while giving generously to charity and providing for both the necessities and the fun activities of life. The financial freedom they enjoyed enabled them to give even more to those in need, to live and travel debt-free, to enjoy golden years of financial dignity instead of near-poverty, and to focus more attention on the deeper, more important issues of life. They had chosen the road less traveled, the road of surer footing.

What is the road less traveled? Why is it that, among people of similar incomes, some enjoy financial freedom while others teeter just three weeks from bankruptcy? The answer is the key point I want you to walk away with today, for it is foundational to your journey to financial freedom:

It's not how much you make but *what you do with* what you make.

Which is, in a nutshell, what this book is all about.

If Jeff and MaryAnn's situation is like yours, you can take heart. (At least your parents didn't name you Northcote.) Jeff and MaryAnn turned their finances around by applying the same sound-money strategies you're going to discover on our journey together. They did so without a dramatic increase in income. It didn't really matter how much money they made. What did they do? They returned to the fork in the road and chose the better path. It was *what they did with what they made* that made all the difference.

And so it will be for you.

LESSON OF THE DAY

"More money" isn't the answer to my financial problems. It's what I do with my money that will make all the difference.

DAY 2

The Dirty Dozen

Twelve reasons why good people fail with their money

A t first, it doesn't make much sense at all. On one side of the street live Jack and Jill, parents of 2.3 rambunctious young children. Jack and Jill earn nearly $80,000 combined income but seem to barely squeak by from paycheck to paycheck. Their savings are minimal, their consumer debt staggering, and every month they find themselves counting the days to the next payday. *If only we made more money,* they reason, *we could get on top of our finances.*

On the other side of the street are Tom and Sally, also the parents of 2.3 rambunctious young children. Tom and Sally earn $47,000 combined income. Yet they've managed to build a significant savings reserve, start an investment portfolio, give generously to their church, and keep credit cards under control. They live comfortably and still have funds remaining in their checking account when payday arrives.

It seems to defy logic: The couple earning less is doing fine, while the "richer" couple can't seem to get their financial act together. Most financial planners will attest to the fact that this scenario is played out in more neighborhoods than you might imagine. Could it be happening on your street, in a family to whom you feel especially close?

What makes the difference between the family that struggles from paycheck to paycheck and the family that enjoys financial freedom?

Luck? No, Tom and Sally didn't inherit Uncle Luigi's pasta empire, because they don't have an Uncle Luigi. They haven't played Lotto and don't plan to. Everything they have, they've earned through their own hard work—and some smart money moves.

It all comes down to the choices we make as we go through life, to how we apply some basic but vital rules of personal financial management. Since our objective is to identify bad habits and change them into good habits, we're going to overview the rules by seeing what happens when they're *not* heeded—twelve big reasons why good, well-intentioned people fail with their money. Let's call them the Dirty Dozen.

How many of these financial *faux pas* describe your way with money?

THE DIRTY DOZEN

1. Lack of specific, measurable goals

It's a funny thing: The chances of reaching a destination are dramatically enhanced if you have a destination in mind. To put it another way—if you aim at nothing, you're bound to hit it. Without specific, measurable financial goals, you lack the roadmap needed to guide you on your journey to financial freedom. Consequently, it's far too easy to stray off the path to all those nowhere towns named Spendthrift, Goosechase Gulch, or Snakebit Junction.

Clear goals, on the other hand, will help you make wiser decisions whenever those exit signs beckon you from the chosen path. You'll cruise past the pitfalls because you have the big picture, the destination, in view. But this doesn't mean you won't have fun along the way—people with specific, measurable financial goals find that their lives are usually in better balance day to day as well as over the long haul.

2. Longing for More Money

One of the easiest traps to fall into is thinking that the solution to our money problems is simply More Money. Ask most people how much money it would take to make them feel better about their finances; no matter how much they make (could be millions) their answer is inevitably, "Just a little more than I make now. Then I could pay my bills, get out of debt, and save for the future."

Well, More Money may or may not be in your future. Most likely it will, especially after you complete this program. However, as we saw yesterday, *Expenditures rise to meet income*. If this is indeed true, then More Money really isn't the answer. The secret lies in having a deep sense of gratitude for whatever does come our way, then expressing that gratitude by managing those funds more shrewdly to achieve our goals.

3. Holding money too loosely

Let's face it: Society tends to measure success and "worth" by the quality and quantity of our possessions. Our grandparents' counsel to save for a rainy day, to save and pay cash for a big purchase, and to live within our means has caved to today's more "enlightened" standard of having it all now by simply using our easy-to-get credit. Why wait when we can take it home tonight? Why not have a car for every driver in the house, plus a truck for good measure?

A big reason many people long for More Money is that, in a normal month, they typically spend most, all, or more than they bring in. They hold their money too loosely, spending without a plan as though the world ends tomorrow. Why not go out to dinner again tonight? Cash is short, but there's always Master-Card.

4. Misusing consumer credit

That's right, there's *always* MasterCard. With its hand out. And Visa, and Discover, and dozens of other convenient ways to get into trouble. Run up your balance and MasterCard is *always* there, helping you "Buy Now, Pay Forever."

Financial counselors estimate that we spend 30 percent more when using credit cards than when we use cash. Misuse of consumer credit is arguably the most dastardly of the Dirty Dozen because it robs your future to pay for your past. It is so epidemic that we're going to devote five full days to helping you get rid of debt and stay debt-free for good. There are much better things you can do with that money, such as making a generous donation to the "Benson to Burmuda" fund.

5. Holding money too tightly

Though filthy rich, Ebenezer Scrooge was the most crotchety old cuss in London. Scrooge hoarded every crown, pound, and shilling, refusing to spend for more than bare necessity. And share with those less fortunate? Humbug! To this day, Charles Dickens' classic character is the quintessential symbol for miserly misery. Though wealthy, Scrooge was not financially free. He was rich in money but poor in spirit—until he learned that real wealth could come only when he was willing to let go. Then, and only then, would he be financially free.

Scrooge discovered the joy of sharing and giving, that people come before pence, that money serves us only when we cease serving money. Financial self-centeredness leads only to an insular, lonely life. A generous spirit, on the other hand, helps us remember the significance of others as precious souls created, valued, and loved by God.

6. Failing to save systematically for the future

"But I just don't have anything left to save!" It's a common lament. Life's tough. It ain't cheap. And besides, we really needed that new speedboat.

When we fail to save systematically, we guarantee that we will be unprepared for the inevitable emergencies and needs of the future. Which means that if we cannot handle those circumstances from our monthly cash flow, we must borrow to meet those needs, digging ourselves deeper into the quagmire of debt. Systematic savings provides a cushion for such emergencies. It also is the key to being ready for future expenses such as a more reliable car, our children's college education, or retirement.

Aye, there's the rub. Saving is important. No, vital. No, *crucial*. Yet it's often the most commonly procrastinated, poorly managed part of our financial lives. If systematic saving has been a problem for you, we'll change that. (And if you've been saving it, we'll show you how to do even better.)

7. Poor management of savings, if any

Okay. Many people have built up some degree of savings, whether systematically or sporadically. But then looms the next money trap: poor management of those savings. It rears its homely head in several ways. Maybe you settle for pathetic rates of interest. Or perhaps you save mostly to spend, like a pubescent teen who works after school, weekends, and all summer so he can go to . . . Cary's Corvette Corner. Once that Vette is his, he's back to square one with savings, and far less likely to rebuild it because of sky-high car and insurance payments.

Yes, saving to spend can be wise as long as it's not our sole savings strategy. The important, vital, crucial part is that we also think long-term. And that requires smart stewardship on our part.

8. Poor insurance choices

Insurance coverage can be healthy or hideous. Healthy, when you purchase wisely to protect against loss of important assets. Hideous, if you either *under*insure (and expose important assets to undue risk) or *over*insure (and waste hundreds, sometimes thousands, of good dollars on inefficient or unnecessary coverage). Financial failure can happen either way, though the first is more catastrophic. The second is more subtle, like a quiet flush of your money down the toilet.

9. Unsavvy car purchases

We've all heard how much a new automobile depreciates within a nanosecond of leaving the car lot. Yet we continue paying the big, big bucks for the temporary pleasure of that new-car smell. Combine rapid depreciation with hefty price, expensive add-ons, fees and finance charges, and the way we typically buy a car may be the single biggest waste of good money in our lives. We can misspend thousands of dollars on a single car; tens of thousands over a lifetime.

10. Paying more to Uncle than required

As citizens who enjoy many blessings of the Land of the Free, we should pay our fair share of taxes graciously. But there is nothing moral or patriotic about paying more than the law mandates. Our Uncle Sam may love it when we pay him more than he requires, but let's face it: Overpayment of taxes is lousy stewardship. The United States is burdened with a Rube-Goldberg tax code that absolutely no one can explain, not even its writers, because they're either dead or institutionalized. Call the IRS helpline and, if they answer, they'll give you directions to Mongolia. The tax code gets crazier every time Congress simplifies it, and printing it has used up every tree in the rain forest. Which is why the IRS has turned its eye to Mongolia. I once tried to figure out the tax code, but I lost my mind. (I've been much happier without it.)

We'll address some of the most dynamic ways for you to save taxes during our 21 days together. For more complex tax issues you'll want to consult a full-time tax professional, whose guess is as good as anyone's.

11. Failing to provide adequately for loved ones

Perhaps the most sobering verse in the Bible for the family provider is 1 Timothy 5:8: "If anyone does not provide for his relatives, and especially for his immediate family, he has denied the faith and is worse than an unbeliever." Strong language, but a strong subject.

Few of us would consciously neglect to provide food, clothing, shelter, and other essentials for our families on an ongoing basis. We provide because we love our families and care deeply about their well-being. But what about future provision? If you were to suddenly leave this earth, have you taken steps to be sure your spouse and children's financial needs will be met in your absence? What if you were disabled, unable to work? What about your retirement years? Do you have strategies in place to provide for those future needs?

Which leads us to . . .

12. Failing to think long-term

The path to financial freedom involves journeying with the destination, not just the next step, in mind. This means managing our money for the long-term as well as the immediate future. You may know some dear folk who have reached the senior stage of life but have little to call their own. As a result, they live in near-poverty during what should be some of the most joy-filled years of their lives. They may need to continue working at whatever employment they can find. Or move in with their children. Or depend solely on Social Security—a safety net with some huge holes in it.

Wouldn't you like to reach retirement age with your financial ducks in a row—able to live, travel, recreate, and volunteer as you want to? While you deal with the everyday challenges of personal finance, be sure to plan, save, and invest for the long-term as well. We'll explore some sound strategies to help you do so.

BACK ON THE PATH

Do any of the Dirty Dozen describe your financial life?

If so, which ones?

If not, which planet are you *really* from?

If you got nailed by one or more of the Dirty Dozen, please don't be discouraged. During the next 19 days we're going to correct the missteps. We'll see what went wrong, regroup, and get back on the path to financial freedom. Scout's honor.

Sound good?

See you tomorrow.

LESSON OF THE DAY

The Dirty Dozen traps that tend to hold me back most are: _____, _____, and _____. But just you watch: I'm going to break free of them during the next 19 days!

DAY 3

First, Give Some Away

The first step to financial freedom is letting go

Ah, 'tis a strange paradox. But so true. We experience it at Christmas, birthdays, special occasions. Or when we give a gift for no particular reason at all. When we give, we show others we love and appreciate them. That they are special to us. That we're grateful for the friendship, love, and joy they bring to our lives.

But that's where the paradox comes through: While giving is intended to bless the receiver, it usually blesses the giver, too. And sometimes far more.

Talk to two people of equal income and wealth. One hoards her money, fearful of letting any of it leave her white-knuckled grasp. The other, a responsible saver and steward, is also a generous giver. Who is happier? Which woman has a deeper level of joy? Peace? And freedom?

It is a paradox, but one that has proven itself over and over again, through the ages and in our time: It is more blessed to give than to receive. Receiving's fun, but giving's funner!

THE JOY OF GIVING

Our Lord Jesus Christ made the joy of giving so clear:

> Give, and it will be given to you. A good measure, pressed down, shaken together and running over, will be poured into your lap. For with the measure you use, it will be measured to you. (Luke 6:38)

Jesus always used real-life word pictures to illustrate his teaching. Here he wants you to imagine that you've just given a large basket of food to someone in need—not out of coercion or obligation but from an unselfish, grateful heart. Will your gift deplete your cupboards? Leave you hungry? No. Imagine sitting down, holding the large, now-empty basket in your lap. Because of your generous gift, he now fills your basket to the brim. Shake it to make more room, and the blessings continue, to the point of overflowing. You now have what you need for today, something to set aside for tomorrow, and more to give— a good measure, pressed down, shaken together, and running over!

Giving is sharing the blessings of God. It is an indication of the honor we give him in our lives, of our gratitude for his provision, and of our obedience to his commands to care for those less fortunate and help spread his message around the world. Thus, the first step to financial freedom is to let go. Even if there were nothing more to it, helping others in God's name is a joyful, complete, fulfilling discipline. He doesn't need the money, but he knows we need to give.

Yet we can't escape the paradox:

> One man gives freely, yet gains even more;
> another withholds unduly,
> but comes to poverty.
> A generous man will prosper;

he who refreshes others will
himself be refreshed.
(Proverbs 11:24–25)

A generous man will prosper. He who refreshes others will himself be refreshed. Give, and it shall be given to you. It's a promise, and a fact. As we give, we receive. We can't out-bless God. Yet our motivation cannot be to receive, for then we miss the outrageous blessing of giving simply because God created us to give.

Is this fun, or what?

GIVE IN THE FIRST PLACE

Where, on your list of financial priorities, do you place the act of regular, unselfish giving? Some people have little room for it, other than a few discards to Goodwill and perhaps a few bucks at Christmastime. Other well-intentioned but unorganized souls give a bit here, a bit there, from the remainders of their income, if any. But giving, to be truly beneficial to others and liberating to ourselves, can't be an afterthought, for then it happens only in the unlikely event that we have something left after attending to our monthly needs and greeds. To experience the true joy of giving, we must make sure we give in the first place, before we do anything else with our money. King Solomon, who was even richer than Bill Gates, said it this way:

Honor the LORD from your wealth, and from the *first* of all your produce. (Proverbs 3:9, NASB, emphasis added)

GIVE CHEERFULLY

Remember this: Whoever sows sparingly will also reap sparingly, and whoever sows generously will also reap generously. Each man should give what he has decided in his heart to give, not reluctantly or under compulsion, for God loves a cheerful giver (2 Corinthians 9:6–7).

In the original language of New Testament Scripture, which is Greek to me, the word for "cheerful" is *hilaros,* from which we get the English word *hilarious.* Be a hilarious giver? You bet. This isn't *Days of Our Lives* or some other soap opera where a lead character always has amnesia. God wants our giving to be a cheerful, delightful act. One that brings a smile to our face. When we give from a happy heart, we're saying how grateful we are for all God has given us. If we smile as we give, so will he.

GIVE FAITHFULLY

The cheerful giver makes sure that regular giving is a priority by making a *tithe*, or a commitment of a percentage of income right off the top. God makes no demands about specific amounts. Most Christians follow the example of a group in the Old Testament, who gave the first one-tenth of their produce to the Lord's work. Many enjoy giving much more, with a calm assurance that God will be faithful in meeting their needs.

If you have discovered the delightful paradox of giving money away, you know the joy we've been talking about. Keep it going! If you're new to this, let me encourage you to make giving off the top of your income a new priority in your financial and spiritual journey. Determine a specific percentage of every paycheck, or of each month's total income, to give to your church or favorite charitable organization. Write the check(s) first, not last, to signify the new priority of giving in your life.

GIVE WISELY

We've all seen and read stories of unfortunate folk who have been "taken" by fraudulent charities. I recently received a cordial call from a "police auxiliary" organization allegedly raising funds to support "our men behind the badge." Now I may not be the brightest guy in the world, but I didn't just fall off the kumquat truck, either. I told the caller I never give over the phone but would be happy to review some literature if he'd like to send it. He never did. Coupla weeks later the newspaper announced that a fraudulent charity had been calling people "on behalf of the local police."

One guideline Kathy and I established years ago is that *we will never give or buy in response to a phone call from someone we don't know.* Same holds true for door-to-door solicitors, except for those cherubic kids selling Girl Scout cookies or candy for a school fundraiser.

Give thoughtfully and carefully. Support your local church and ministries or charities of good repute.

GIVE QUIETLY

The ultimate purpose of giving is to glorify God, not ourselves. Again, the words of his Son:

> Be careful not to do your "acts of righteousness" before men, to be seen by them. If you do, you will have no reward from your Father in heaven.
>
> So when you give to the needy, do not announce it with trumpets, as the hypocrites do in the synagogues and on the streets, to be honored by men. I tell you the truth, they have received their reward in full. But when you give to the needy, do not let your left hand know what your right hand is doing, so that your giving may be in secret. Then your Father, who sees what is done in secret, will reward you. (Matthew 6:1–4)

It's human nature to want to "let it slip" that we give X dollars here, X dollars there. That we sent Chuck and Melinda some money during a recent financial crisis. Contrary to human nature, God wants us to give quietly . . . from a gracious, thankful heart that longs to give him the glory.

At first you may wonder how you can give off the top and meet your other obligations. Trust me, you can do it. That's why it's a paradox. Give cheerfully, faithfully, wisely, and quietly . . . and the rest will fall into place. Like a good measure, pressed down, shaken together, and running over.

LESSON OF THE DAY

First, I will give some away.

DAY 4

Found Money!

You may already have more money than you think

Okay, you caught me.

"Hey," you said, smartly picking up on the title and subtitle of this chapter, "on Day 1 you told me that More Money isn't really the answer to my financial problems. Now here you are talking about More Money. You can't have it both ways."

My answer to that is the classic rebuttal often used by famed trial attorney Clarence Darrow: "Oh, yeah?"

More Money may not be the answer, but I never said it wouldn't help. Unbeknownst to you, but knownst to me, you could have several hundred dollars—perhaps several *thousand*—available that you didn't know about.

THE SWEET SURPRISE

The business world has a term that's music to every corporate leader's ears: *Found Money*. It's used to describe newly discovered dollars the company didn't realize it had, or cash that becomes available when a planned expense is no longer necessary. Found Money is always a sweet surprise.

Found Money happens in personal finance as well. Remember the day you discovered the $10 bill you had tucked away in your wallet and forgotten? Okay, maybe you haven't been *that* fortunate. How about the day you vacuumed under the chair cushion and found a quarter, a dime, and half a tortilla chip? All right, if you've never vacuumed under the cushion, have you ever received a refund of an overpayment? Or of a security deposit you forgot about? Or thought you might owe $400 in taxes but ended up owing only $23?

You may be thinking, *Well, that never happens to me. I'm the poster child for Lost Money. The only financial surprises I have are when the car breaks down or the furnace blows up. Why can't I come across some Found Money?* Not so fast. You just might. In fact, I can almost guarantee it.

If money has seemed tight lately, you may indeed wonder where the money's going to come from to get out of debt, build your savings, and prepare for an independent retirement. These are normal qualms, whether you're normal or not. So our purpose today is to assure you that you probably have more money than you think and to help you find it.

EMPTY YOUR POCKETS

I don't know about you, but I hate counting out change when I buy something; I'd rather save time and hand the clerk a dollar bill and let him make change. I'm sure a psychologist would have fun with this—Repressed Post-Traumatic Regressive Disorder or something, and probably my mother's fault. Regardless, most evenings I come home with enough loose change to fund all the parking meters in the city.

How about you? Even if you don't have Repressed Post-Whatever, you likely accumulate plenty of loose change. Let's say that on a typical day you return home with three quarters, a dime, two nickels, and three pennies: 98 cents. Some days you'll have more, some days less, so let's consider 98 cents an average day.

Starting tonight, whenever you get home from work or shopping or an evening out, empty your pocket or purse of all the coins you've accumulated. Place them in a hermetically sealed mayonnaise jar and watch what happens. Ninety-eight cents per day adds up to $6.86 in one week. At the end of one month, your 98 cents per day will have metamorphosed into a beautiful $30 or so. That adds up to $360 per year, *before interest*. Not bad for money which, till now, mostly fell through the cracks.

If you want, you can stop at loose change when emptying your pockets. But just for the fun of it, what would happen if you add just *one* of the dollar bills in your pocket, wallet, or purse each evening? The $1.98 total is still less than the price of a cup of coffee, which at press time was about $3 at the local gourmet shop and $100,000 at the Clinton White House. In a week $1.98 becomes $13.86. In a month it's $61.38. In a year it's $722.70. See where this is headed? Found Money!

Once each month, take the mayonnaise jar to your bank. Don't be embarrassed—they have machines to sort and count change. Tell the nice teller that your lemonade stand is doing very nicely, thank you. Deposit the total in your checking account, then earmark this Found Money to monthly priorities such as savings, debt reduction, increased giving, investments.

It's a painless, effective strategy. The only requirements: patience and loose change. I know couples who virtually funded their children's college education in this way. Over time, those little handfuls of pocket change can add up to thousands of dollars.

SELL SOME STUFF

What do you have sitting around that you can sell? Okay, other than the husband? Is there an extra vehicle that's draining cash, that's not (really) necessary? How about a motorcycle, a bike, skis, in-line skates, exercise equipment, or CD or video player? Grown tired of a TV set, or a CD or video collection? All of us have too much Stuff—things we-just-had-ta-have but no longer use or need. It may as well be cluttering someone else's basement.

Survey your place for at least two items you could sell for $100 or more. Then call your local classifieds and put flyers on your bulletin boards at work. You also may discover that you've accumulated enough Stuff to stage a profitable garage sale. Found Money!

STOP LOANING TO YOUR GREEDY UNCLE

Pssst—have I got a deal for you. The XYZ Company is a huge organization in need of capital. If you loan them some of your money from each paycheck, whether it's $20 or $200, they'll take that money and put it to work. By the end of the year, you'll have contributed hundreds, maybe thousands, to the program. A few months later, XYZ Company will return your money to you. And to show their deep appreciation for the loan, they will also give you an exciting return on investment of (are you ready for this?) *absolutely nothing*. That's right, you loaned XYZ your hard-earned money, they used it all year, and they paid you *zero interest!*

Now if someone approached you with this benevolent offer, I'm confident you'd give him a benevolent kick out the door. It just doesn't make sense to give XYZ interest-free loans from each paycheck when you can invest those dollars yourself, realizing gains of between 5 and 20 percent each year.

Would you believe XYZ Company is a real organization? And that the majority of Americans unwittingly make that horrid interest-free loan from every paycheck? By now you know which organization I'm talking about; I just misspelled the initials. It's *IRS*. Our friendly federal tax collector, a.k.a. Uncle Sam, last seen pickpocketing along Main Street, considered armed and extremely dangerous. And if you received a tax refund last spring, you made him that same zero-interest loan.

Now I realize it's usually a nice feeling when a refund check arrives. But consider the big picture: A tax refund simply means you're letting Uncle overwithhold your taxes each payday; you're paying him more than he requires of you. Each overpayment is a virtual loan of your hard-earned money to Uncle Sam at *zero interest*.

If last year's refund was less than a couple hundred dollars and your financial situation hasn't changed much, you may want to leave things as they are. But if your refund was more than a few hundred, you may be able to turn your zilch-interest loans into Found Money. The payroll specialist at your workplace has IRS tables to help you calculate a new withholding allowance. You can take up to 10 allowances rather simply; more than 10 requires tedious paperwork pledging your children, jewelry, and family dog to assure Uncle you're not going to stiff him and flee to Argentina.

Increasing your withholding allowances is a simple, effective way to turn those going-nowhere IRS loans into Found Money. It can provide more dollars each pay period to direct toward investments that work for *your* benefit instead of Uncle's. You won't have a huge tax refund next spring, but that's just the point. Your goal is to come close to "break-even" at tax time by putting your money to wiser use in the meantime.

GET RID OF BAD LIFE INSURANCE

If you're among the millions who let a hungry insurance salesman sell you *whole life* insurance, chances are we've stumbled upon a key source of Found Money. Unless you are over age 50 and a smoker, or suffer from serious chronic illness, it's likely that whole life (also called *permanent life*) is not a good insurance buy for you. In fact, it can be one of the worst investments foisted upon the public.

The pitch is that in addition to life insurance coverage, you will build *cash value* in a sort of savings fund, and you can borrow this cash value at any time. Salesmen push whole life for two reasons: higher premiums to the company and higher commissions to the salesmen. "Won't it be great to have a 'forced savings' program to build your savings while you're providing for your loved ones?" he/she asks. "This is one of the safest investments you can make."

Be still, my heart.

With whole life insurance, or most of its derivatives such as *variable life* or *universal life,* you're paying an enormous premium for relatively little insurance coverage. Almost all of your first year's premium for whole life coverage goes to the salesman as commission—little if any goes to cash value. In fact, it takes a few years for your cash value to begin showing signs of life at all.

You can borrow from the cash value in your policy, and you don't have to pay it back if you don't want to. Sound pretty good? Here's the really good part: *If you should die after borrowing your cash value, the life insurance proceeds to your beneficiary will be reduced by the outstanding amount of the loan.* Well, that's a bummer, but maybe it's only fair since you borrowed the money and won't be paying it back. But wait: *The money was yours in the first place.* Your beneficiaries will be short-changed because you borrowed back your own money. Bottom line: While there may be a few, rare situations in which which whole life is appropriate (consult your advisor), in most cases cash value life insurance is little more than a deliberate overcharge and overpayment of premiums.

The basic principle here is that insurance is insurance and investments are investments, and we shouldn't heed the hype to combine the two. You'll likely do much better shopping for inexpensive *term insurance,* which buys you far more insurance at a far lower cost-per-thousand of coverage. The difference between term and what you will pay for whole life could total hundreds, *perhaps thousands,* of dollars per year—Found Money you can invest on your own without exorbitant commissions or fees, and come out far ahead. We'll suggest some good sources of term life insurance on Day 19.

PROVIDE A SERVICE

Perhaps you have a special skill or service you can sell in your spare time: carpentry, babysitting, house cleaning, handyperson work, typing, computer setup or lessons, photography. Maybe you're adept at writing, editing, or proofreading, or you can design a killer brochure on your computer. If you're a musician, could you offer singing lessons or teach a musical instrument? (If you're a lousy musician, could you offer to *not* sing?) Are you good at plumbing or auto repair? How about yard maintenance or sprinkler system startup and shutoff? Snow shoveling or hanging Christmas lights?

If you can name it, you can make money at it. Place ads on bulletin boards at work, print a flyer for your neighborhood, and tell friends and neighbors you're available for a fair sum. Found money!

CONSIDER REFINANCING

Paying a mortgage? If interest rates have fallen since you secured your loan, or if you have an adjustable rate mortgage that's about to adjust you out of your home, and if you plan on staying in your home at least three more years, you may be a candidate for refinancing your home loan.

Let me suggest you call at least five mortgage lenders in your area to check their fees as well as their present rate on a 30-year fixed mortgage. One national lender that is historically competitive is Countrywide; they're in most phone books. But talk to other mortgage lenders too—local and national. Depending on the current economy and your specific situation, you may be able to refinance your mortgage and significantly reduce your monthly principal and interest payments. The difference? Found Money.

ACCELERATE YOUR MORTGAGE PRINCIPAL

If you anticipate staying in your house a long time, possibly even paying it off and owning it free and clear, here's a strategy that's virtually a sure bet to save you tens of thousands of dollars over the next 15–20 years: *Send extra money to your mortgage company each month and designate it "additional principal."*

Here's how it works: Most mortgage companies provide a space on their monthly bill or coupon for you to send additional principal *if you want to.* If your mortgage company does not offer this option, contact them and ask how you can make additional payments toward your principal. Then, starting next month, write your mortgage check for an additional $50, $100, $150, or more. Specify on the bill or coupon the additional amount that goes to principal.

What this does is accelerate the reduction of the principal balance on which you owe interest. Depending on the size of your mortgage, how long you've had it, your interest rate, and the amount of additional principal you send each month, you can trim 7, 10, 13 years off your payment schedule and save tens of thousands, possibly into the *hundreds of thousands,* in interest on the loan. Found Money?

This prepayment strategy is even more powerful when you systematize it. Have your lender print an *amortization schedule* itemizing the dollar amount of principal and the amount of interest for each month of the loan. (You can run amortization schedules yourself with financial software such as Quicken®.) Then, along with each month's mortgage payment, send an additional amount equal to *next month's principal payment*. Keep in mind that this does not allow you to skip a payment; it's simply a method of private bookkeeping to help you systematically prepay your mortgage in less time. Do this every month and you'll virtually cut the remaining life of your loan in half—saving even more thousands in interest.

MORE ALONG THE WAY

So, do you forgive me for finding you some extra money?

We've touched on some of the most obvious and accessible sources, but be assured we won't stop here. In coming weeks you will discover more good sources of money-you-didn't-realize-you-had, whether it's from clearing debt, or buying smarter, or saving and investing more diligently. Your Found Money could total thousands of dollars before we're through. Like a good measure, pressed down, shaken together, and running over?

LESSON OF THE DAY

I probably have more money than I think. I will stay alert for Found Money, then use it wisely.

Now, Move to the Front of the Line

The most powerful (and ignored) secret of financial freedom

- Ol' Faithful, the car you had hoped to keep alive for three more years, has just gasped, clutched its chest, and died. Suddenly you're looking at new cars, wondering how you're going to handle a down payment and exorbitant monthly payments.
- Your twin sons, Alas and Alak, love roller hockey and have just slapshot a puck through your neighbor's dual-pane picture window. Your checkbook's running low till payday, but you need to replace your neighbor's window *right now.*
- Your pediatrician orders a hospital stay for your daughter, complete with tests, surgery, and $25-per-tissue Kleenex. Your daughter's fine now, but when all the paperwork has settled, you're stuck with several thousand dollars in deductibles and co-payments.

- The boss has a somber look. "Close the door," he says as you enter his office. "I'm deeply sorry, but as you know we're going through a tough time here at Wendel's Widget Wonderland. We have to let you go. There's a party in half an hour."

CERTAINTIES, UNCERTAINTIES

Emergencies. Unexpected expenses. Sudden loss of income. At some point in our lives most of us will encounter scenarios like the ones above. We've been around the block enough times to know that current income does not always meet current expenses. Life's surprises just do not time themselves to fit neatly within our monthly cash flow.

And then there are future financial events that should come as no surprise, but often do. Like the kids' college education. Or a wedding. Or a much-needed, well-deserved vacation. Or retirement—when a steady paycheck is suddenly replaced by a gold watch. These certainties of life, combined with the inevitable uncertainties, underscore the importance of building an accessible financial reserve through a disciplined savings program.

DO YOU LEAVE SAVINGS TO "SOMEDAY"?

Americans are not the most prudent of savers. The average United States household sets aside only 4.9 percent of its after-tax earnings, and the average affluent household saves only about 8.5 percent. Compare our savings habits with those of the Japanese, who typically save between 15 and 20 percent of earnings, and it's clear that setting aside a portion of our income for the future has not been high on our list.

Recently United States savings figures have begun inching upward, primarily because aging Baby Boomers are realizing the need to save more aggressively for approaching retirement. Yet, despite a stronger motive, many of us continue to find excuses to leave saving to "someday." Do any of these sound familiar to you?

- "I'll start saving when I get my next raise."
- "When I get my debts paid off."
- "After the first of the year, when Christmas is over."
- "We've got some stuff we've been wanting to get."
- "We just don't have anything left to save!"
- "Someday, when my ship comes in . . ."

In the short run, procrastination can only lead to further debt and difficulty when we're required to face emergencies and other expenses with little in reserve. In the long run, procrastination can compound to near-destitution during what are supposed to be the "golden years" of life. Financial planners estimate that most of us will need 70 to 80 percent of our pre-retirement income during retirement years. Where will this money come from? Social Security—intended as an absolute-minimum safety net, not a retirement program—will provide only a few hundred dollars per month. You may have a company pension, but even that may prove inadequate to see you through 15 to 25 years of retirement. You might be able to bum off your adult children, but that's comparable to running a marathon with an ingrown toenail.

HANDLE FUTURE SURPRISES WITHOUT DEBT

And let's be realistic: Retirement isn't the only time of life when a financial reserve is necessary. Every one of us can look forward to one or more of the following:

- Down payment on your first house
- Vacations
- Down payments on new cars

- Replenishment of wardrobes
- Children's college expenses
- Children's weddings
- Medical and dental expenses
- Leaves of absence
- Care for ill or elderly parents
- Annual, semi-annual, or quarterly insurance premiums
- Home maintenance and repairs
- Car maintenance and repairs
- Household appliance repair or replacement
- Furniture or decor upgrades
- A friend or ministry in need of financial help
- Christmas, birthdays, anniversaries
- Business opportunities
- Business losses
- Investment opportunities
- Loss of income due to layoff or disability

You may be experiencing some of these circumstances right now. As long as you can fog a mirror, *count on* some of them visiting you in the future. Perhaps this is why the writer of Proverbs stated with such conviction:

> The wise man saves for the future, but the foolish man spends whatever he gets. . . . A prudent man foresees the difficulties ahead and prepares for them; the simpleton goes blindly on and suffers the consequences. (Proverbs 21:20; 22:3 TLB)

Wouldn't you like to handle these situations without having to go into debt? Your chances of doing so will be dramatically enhanced if you begin now to invest a portion of every dollar you earn for your future.

I know, I know. You're thinking, *But you don't know my situation! With my budget, there just isn't anything left to save!* It's a common frustration. Let's face it: It *is* tough out there. Costs don't go down, they go up. Expenditures rise to meet or surpass income. How is it possible to put money in savings when the demand always seems to outstrip the supply?

MOVE TO THE FRONT OF THE LINE

Because of a high level of personal spending, most individuals and couples regard personal savings, like regular giving, as an afterthought. We tend to pay out first for all of our monthly expenses, including debt service, then see if there is anything left for savings. But the key to savings success is to reverse this procedure. Instead of forking out all our funds to expenses and then saying, "Savings? Are you kidding me?" we route a specific percentage of our income to savings *before we pay any other bills.*

In other words, just as we did with the practice of giving on Day 3, we move personal savings from afterthought to priority. After you've given some money away, *Move to the Front of the Line!* You have now become your number one creditor. It's called "Pay Yourself First," and it's the key to diligently setting something aside for the future, regardless of your other expenses, and being prepared for emergencies, needs, and dreams.

Move to the front of the line.

Pay yourself first.

Hey, no back-talk. You *can* do it. Truth is, you *gotta* do it. And you will.

Tomorrow, you'll see how.

LESSON OF THE DAY

*After giving, I will move to the front of the
line and pay myself first.*

DAY 6

Save Automatically

How to make sure you Pay Yourself First instead of last

Yesterday we highlighted the importance of systematic savings and how to make sure it happens: After your top priority of giving, you're next! Move to the front of the line.

If you haven't been giving off the top and Paying Yourself First, these new disciplines may take some adjustment. I wouldn't be honest if I didn't tell you the first month or two might feel tight. But don't give up. If you stay resolute, you will discover that your budget soon molds itself around your new priorities. Within six months, you won't even miss the dollars that are routed to giving and savings.

And when it comes to Paying Yourself First we can ensure that we move to the front of the line by saving *automatically,* thus avoiding the temptation to spend every dollar in sight. Today you'll see two powerful strategies to help you make systematic savings happen automatically. Before we go there, let's take a moment to kick the tires of the vehicle we're going to use: the *money market fund.*

THE BETTER SAVINGS ACCOUNT

A money market fund is a type of mutual fund that invests conservatively in an array of short-term vehicles such as certificates of deposit, commercial paper, and United States government securities. The better ones will bring you higher returns than a bank savings account while maintaining your need for liquidity and preservation of principal. Unlike regular mutual funds, where your principal fluctuates according to market demand, a money market fund maintains the value of your original investment and pays monthly dividends on the earnings of its portfolio. It is not a guaranteed or insured savings vehicle, but its investments are typically so conservative, short-term, and diversified that financial experts deem it just as safe, and probably safer, than an insured bank account. If you're in a high tax bracket, you can choose a tax-free fund.

The money market fund you use will come with free check-writing privileges, usually for a minimum amount ranging from $100 to $500, and the option of making automatic deposits on a biweekly or monthly basis. It will require a minimum initial deposit of $500 to $1000 or more (sometimes waived if you sign for the automatic deposit) and minimum subsequent deposits of $50 or more. You won't want to use it for everyday check writing; maintain your local checking account for that. But your money market fund will serve you well as a convenient, disciplined vehicle for systematic savings.

Money market funds are typically part of a *mutual fund family,* adding extra convenience when you're ready to shift some of your savings into higher-risk, higher-reward vehicles such as stock and bond mutual funds. Hundreds of mutual fund families clamor for our savings and investment dollars. Among the best are:

- The Vanguard Group (Prime Reserve Portfolio) 800–662–7447
- American Century Investments (Benham Cash Reserve) 800–345–2021 or 816–531–5575
- Fidelity Investments (Cash Reserves) 800–544–6666

Customer service reps at each family will be happy to answer your questions and send you a brochure and application for the fund.

Now that we've looked over our chosen vehicle for systematic savings, we're ready to proceed to the two strategies for making Pay Yourself First a reality in your life.

1. Save It Before You See It.

This is by far the best strategy if your employer is set up to do it for you. Many employers offer a program whereby you can designate a specific amount of each paycheck to be deducted from your paycheck and sent directly to a money market fund. It happens like clockwork and you'll be amazed at how quickly these direct deposits add up, assuming you don't raid your fund every time you have a craving for some new Stuff.

We're not talking yet about tax-advantaged programs such as 401(k)s—on Day 14 we'll see how these virtually turbocharge the Pay Yourself First principle. Today we're addressing *liquid savings* you can access if you need to. So check with your payroll person to see if your organization will direct-deposit a specified sum to a money market fund, preferably a fund you have chosen.

2. Save It Before You Can Spend It.

If your employer doesn't offer direct deposits to savings, and even if he does, you can arrange an automatic draft from your personal checking account to the money market fund of your choice. You can direct the fund to draft biweekly or monthly, depending on which is more convenient for your cash flow. Your only obligation is to be sure you deduct the specified amount from your checking account ledger by the designated day of the draft. You've avoided temptation by steering a portion of your earnings to savings *automatically*—before you have a chance to spend it!

I remember how Kathy and I discovered this Pay Yourself First strategy. Yes, I remember that far back. (I'm not *that* old, although in dog years I'm dead.) While we've always believed in giving off the top and the importance of savings, our savings were sporadic during the early part of our marriage. It wasn't until we learned about money market funds that we understood the incredible power of the Pay Yourself First principle.

At first we agreed to designate 5 percent of our after-tax income to savings. And I admit it took some adjusting. But after just three months we realized we no longer missed the money that was automatically going to savings. As the amount in our money market fund grew, we were motivated to keep it going and growing. Soon the Pay Yourself First principle enabled us to purchase our first home. As time passed and income grew, we've increased the percentage of income to automatic savings and investment. This isn't to say we haven't had a few financial hiccups along the way. Who hasn't? But Kathy and I can attest to the fact that Paying Yourself First—*automatically*—is the key to having the funds you need when it's time to replace the transmission your car just deposited over three city blocks, make a higher-ticket consumer purchase, fund a needed vacation, and begin investing for the long term. All without having to go into debt at debilitating rates of interest.

CALL 1–800 . . .

Today's assignment: Call the three 800 numbers listed above. Ask about minimum initial deposits, minimum subsequent deposits, free check-writing privileges, and minimum check-writing amounts. Ask for a brochure, a prospectus, and an application.

45

The material will arrive in three to five days. While you wait, determine the amount you will commit to either biweekly or monthly automatic drafts. Try to begin with a minimum of 5 percent of your current take-home pay. If that's too steep under your present circumstances, commit to *something*—$50 per month is better than $0 per month, and $100 is twice as good as $50. Even if cash flow has been tight, it's possible we've already scratched up enough Found Money to help you get going. Eventually you'll be able to increase your automatic savings commitment to 7, 10, 12 percent or more.

Once you've read the material (and please do), select your mutual fund family and fill out the application for the money market fund. You'll be asked to choose between having monthly dividends mailed to you or reinvested in the fund: Choose the *reinvest* option to help your savings grow on a compounded basis. Mail the application with a check for your initial deposit. Beginning the following month, on the day(s) you specify, your new money market fund will automatically draft the specified amount from your checking account. All you have to do is watch it grow.

Continue this strategy as long as you earn income. For good measure, whenever extra income comes your way, get in the habit of sending a healthy portion of that extra money to savings as well. Remember, a portion of all you earn is yours to keep, so Pay Yourself First.

And make it automatic.

LESSON OF THE DAY

Today I will call for a money market fund prospectus and application. I will set it up for automatic drafts once per month or per pay period.

Save Specifically

How to manage short-term savings so the money's there when you need it

You may recall that one of the Dirty Dozen reasons good people fail financially is *poor management of savings*. In other words, even when they manage to save some money, they're soon pulling it right back out to acquire whatever might catch their eye. Just when savings are near depletion, along comes a true need: The truck dies or the plant downsizes, catching these good folk with their finances down.

Which reminds me. Know what happens when you play country music backward? You get your pickup truck back, you get your job back, you get your dog back, and you get your true love back. (However, with wise management of savings, you might be able to avoid losing all them thangs in the first place.)

Today we'll limit our focus to management of *short-term savings*: the after-tax dollars you're Paying Yourself First to a money market fund, as discussed on Days 5 and 6. In a later chapter, Day 14, we'll deal specifically with long-term strategies for the retirement years.

CERTAIN CERTAINTIES

Think for a few moments on the specific types of periodic "certainties" that stroll through your financial life. Do you have quarterly, semi-annual, or annual insurance premiums? Are you planning a future purchase, such as a large appliance, your next car, some furniture? How about vacation? Christmas, birthdays, anniversaries? A down payment for your first home? These are short-term needs you know about in advance, so there's really no good reason to let them create havoc when they roll in. Beginning now, you're going to save in advance for them and enjoy the wonderfully free feeling of knowing the money is there as the need comes due.

CERTAIN UNCERTAINTIES

Now think on the "uncertainties" that could invade your financial life. Perhaps some already have. A sudden, expensive car repair. A large medical co-payment. A startling dip in earnings, or a total cut-off of income. These are *unexpected* short-term needs—we don't know when they'll happen, but odds are one or all of them *will* happen. We don't know what the future holds, thank God, and we need never live in fear or anxiety. But we can and should prepare as best we can to minimize the inevitable financial surprises that lurk around the next bend.

SO, SAVE SPECIFICALLY

In the next few pages I'll outline an effective method to help organize your money-market-fund savings more strategically for the "certain certainties" and the "certain uncertainties" of life. Let's call it Saving Specifically, because that's exactly what we're going to do: anticipate upcoming expenses and save in advance for them.

Pretend your take-home pay totals $2000 per month and you've committed to saving 10 percent of it, or $200 per month. To Pay Yourself First, Automatically, you've completed and returned the money-market-fund application authorizing an automatic draft from your checking account on the 15th of every month.

Now jump in the car, drive to Wal-Mart, greet the greeter, and ask for the office supplies aisle. There you'll pick up a 6-column columnar pad, the kind accountants use. Once home, open the columnar pad so you have a double-page spread. You'll see 6 numbered columns per page, plus a few anonymous columns to their left, so on a double-page spread you'll have 12 numbered columns. At the top of these columns, from column 2 through column 11, write the name of a key *expected* future expense. Immediately under the expense, write the date(s) they will come due. For example, at the top of column 2 you might write: *LIFE INS.* Under which you would put *(Mar. 31, Sept. 31)*. This would indicate semi-annual life insurance premiums due the end of March and the end of September each year.

You may not need all 10 columns (2–11) for expected expenses. But this is where you'll keep track of how much you're setting aside for specific, expected future needs. Use these columns to save for insurance premiums, vacation, planned purchases, gifts, and anything else you anticipate dropping significant bucks on in the next year or two.

Now go to the top of column 12 and write *CONTINGENCY.* This is where you'll keep track of your savings for a big, *unexpected* emergency such as a layoff, a death in the family, or even the death of a much-needed vehicle. These things aren't fun to contemplate, but they're even less fun to experience. Thus, a contingency reserve should be among your top savings priorities. Financial counselors advise building and maintaining a reserve of 3 to 6 months' living expenses to help you through such times.

Shift left to column 1. This is where you'll maintain a running total of all the assets in your money market fund. In other words, the total in column 1 equals the total of columns 2 through 12. Write *FUND TOTAL* in the header box for column 1.

Still moving left, use the large column adjacent to column 1 to make notations of all money market fund transactions, just as you do in your checkbook. Write *TRANSACTION* in the header box atop this column. Left again, you'll see some small boxes next to your new *TRANSACTION* column. You'll use these boxes to indicate the date on which you make a deposit or withdrawal from the money market fund, and to check off a transaction after confirming it against the monthly or quarterly statement your fund will send you.

TEST IT OUT

I'm confident that by now you're beginning to see how helpful Saving Specifically is going to be. Just to be sure, let's do a dry run.

1. Say you sent a check for $200 with your application to open the fund.
2. On line 1 of your tracking sheets, far left, indicate the date of the transaction. Then, staying on line 1 for the transaction:
3. In the next column, *TRANSACTIONS,* write *(D) $200 Initial Deposit.* (Throughout this system you'll indicate *(D)*

for Deposit, (*I*) for Income Reinvest, and (*W*) for With-drawal.)

4. Under column 1, *FUND TOTAL*, write *$200.00*.
5. Now you have the fun of determining where you want this deposit to go. You can split it up among several categories, or steer all of it to one category. For this example, you know you need to start saving for an upcoming annual life insurance premium of $380, and you also believe you should begin building your contingency reserve. You decide on a 50–50 split.
6. Under *LIFE INS.*, write *$100.00*.
7. Under column 12, *CONTINGENCY*, write *$100.00*.
8. Under all other categories, columns 2–11, make a dash indicating balances of zero dollars.

You now have saved $100 toward your upcoming life insurance premium and $100 toward your emergency reserve. See how this is gonna work? On or before the 15th of each month, you'll deduct the $200 automatic draft from your checking account. You'll turn to your new money market fund record and indicate the $200 transfer as a deposit made on the 15th. You'll add it to the *FUND TOTAL*, then apportion it among your savings categories according to your priorities.

Whenever some extra money comes along (Found Money, higher earnings, refunds, and so forth), deposit a good chunk of that to your money market fund as well, again according to your priorities.

In addition to your deposits, your money market fund will earn monthly dividends. On your application form you instructed the trustee to reinvest all dividends to keep them in your accumulated savings. When your monthly or quarterly statement arrives, add these dividend reinvestments to your *FUND TOTAL*, then decide in which category you want them to go. (I suggest the *CONTINGENCY* category to accelerate its progress.)

HOW TO PULL MONEY OUT

When a specific planned expense comes due, how do you pull money out of your money market fund? It's as simple as writing a check, because your money market fund gives you a book of checks and free check writing privileges. (Don't get carried away.) Say your annual life insurance premium is due and you've built $380 in your *LIFE INS.* savings category. Using your money market checkbook, write a check to the insurance company for $380 just as you would a local bank check. It's real money, so it's all the same to your insurance company. You'll then write a dash on the next available line of your *LIFE INS.* column to indicate a new balance of zero, subtract $380 from column 1's *FUND TOTAL,* and describe the transaction in the *TRANSACTION* column: *(W) $380 Life Insurance Premium.*

You may be saying to yourself, *Self, this sure sounds complicated.* Let me assure you, it's not. Practice a few times, keep good records for a month or two, and you'll see what I mean. Saving Specifically is a simple tool to serve *you*—you don't serve *it*. And it's *flexible*. You can change categories and column headings any time. You can shift dollars from one category to another. Best of all, your money-market-fund record maintains at a glance a clear picture of your short-term savings organization and progress. It won't prevent big expenses from rambling into your life, but it'll sure help keep them from knocking you off your feet.

LESSON OF THE DAY

I will manage my short-term savings wisely
by Saving Specifically.

Chart Your Course

The chance of reaching your destination is dramatically increased if you have a destination in mind

How many people do you know who seem to grope through life hoping for an elusive ship to come in "someday," but after several years—sometimes decades—they're perplexed over how little they have to show for their labors? "Where does it all go?" they soliloquize, helplessly shaking their heads.

Almost without exception, men and women who enjoy financial freedom are goal planners. Just as you and I couldn't fathom starting a cross-country trek through unfamiliar territory without a trail map, so we should not undertake a financial journey without knowing the signs to look for to be sure we're on the proper trail. Clear financial goals serve as checkpoints to help guide us past all those energy-draining side trails marked *This Way to Goosechase Gulch*.

AIM AT NOTHING AND YOU'RE BOUND TO HIT IT

In get-acquainted sessions with financial planning clients, we always asked about retirement goals. On more than one occasion the answer went like this: "I'd like to retire someday, with lots of money, and have lots of fun."

Such a goal statement was of little help because it was so vague. Aim at nothing and you're bound to hit it. These clients are like the archer who shoots an arrow into the air, then paints a target around the arrow wherever it lands. Without specific and measurable goals to guide their aim, people with vague goals will someday find themselves near retirement, wondering how they'll ever make it through the last 20 to 30 years of life.

On the other hand, once we knew that a couple would like to retire in 24 years with a paid-for home and a monthly income equal to $3000 in today's dollars, we could formulate a series of integrated financial strategies to help them achieve their goals.

Shorter-term goal setting can and should be just as specific. Instead of longing for "a good vacation someday," decide specifically *when* you want to take the vacation, *how much* money you'll need, and *where the funds might come from* between now and then. If you determine that you want to start the vacation in nine months and that you'll need $2000 for the trip, you can examine your liquid assets and anticipated income sources to formulate a plan for a relaxing, cash-on-the-barrelhead vacation.

GET READY TO DREAM

A goal is a dream with a deadline. That puts the whole process in a nutshell; effective goal planning is the art of identifying your needs and dreams, putting them on paper, prioritizing them, and determining when and how you can best accomplish each one.

Before you begin dreaming, let me suggest you spend some time in prayer, asking God that the desires of his heart would be the desires of your heart. We are told in Psalm 127:1 that unless the Lord builds the house, its builders labor in vain. Fortunately, we're also promised that "If any of you lacks wisdom, he should ask God, who gives generously to all without finding fault, and it will be given to him" (James 1:5).

Prayers said, pen in hand, and lots of blank paper before you, use the following checkpoints of personal finance to stimulate your thinking.

GOAL PLANNING CHECKPOINTS

- What financial freedom looks like to us
  What does financial freedom mean to us today?
  What will it "look like" ten years from now?
  What will it look like as we're nearing retirement?

- Our level of charitable giving
  Currently:
  Within 6–12 months:
  In three years:
  Long-term:

- Our monthly spending habits
  Currently:
  Within 6–12 months:
  In three years:
  Long-term:

- Our consumer debt load
  Currently:
  Within 6–12 months:
  In three years:
  Long-term:

- Our level of liquid reserves for emergencies
Currently:
Within 6–12 months:
In three years:
Long-term:

- Our housing
Currently:
In three years:
Long-term:

- Our protection of assets (level of insurance needed) in the event of:
Death of a breadwinner
  Currently:
  Within 6–12 months:
Long-term disability of a breadwinner
  Currently:
  Within 6–12 months:
Major medical expense
  Currently:
  Within 6–12 months:
Major damage to home and furnishings
  Currently:
  Within 6–12 months:
Auto accidents and liabilities
  Currently:
  Within 6–12 months:
Excess liability coverage
  Currently:
  Within 6–12 months:

- Our savings for future expenses
Currently:
Within 6–12 months:

In three years:
Long-term:

- Our tax-advantaged savings and investments for retirement
  Currently:
  Within 6–12 months:
  In three years:
  Long-term:

- Other investments (stocks, bonds, mutual funds, real estate, Lotto tickets, just kidding about the Lotto tickets)
  Currently:
  Within 6–12 months:
  In three years:
  Long-term:

- Other financial goals (career, education, small business, big trip, hostile takeover of Microsoft and General Motors)
  Within 6–12 months:
  In three years:
  Long-term:

Don't be frustrated if you're unable to cover all these checkpoints in one session. It's a lot to think about, so take your time and spread the process over three or four sessions if necessary. Goal planning is that important!

PRIORITIZE AND SHAPE YOUR GOALS

Now it's time to sharpen your focus a bit.

Prayerfully go through your list and rank your goals, 1 to 20,000, in the order of importance to you. Then take the *Top 5* and rework each of the five into a specific, optimistic goal statement:

We will [goal to be accomplished] *by* [deadline]. *To achieve this goal, we will* [specific action to be taken] *by* [date action is to begin]. [Further resolution here, if needed.]

As an example, let's say you're feeling a tad jumpy with all the downsizing going on around you. You determine that one of your Top 5 goals is to have a total of $3000 set aside as a contingency reserve within a year (and perhaps $9000+ in three years) just in case the Ghost of Unemployment comes knocking. Your present contingency balance is $600, leaving $2400 to attain your one-year goal. Your written goal might read like this:

We will save a total of $3000 in our contingency reserve by [specify date]. *To do so, we will contribute $200 per month by automatic draft from our checking account to our money market fund beginning the 15th of next month. Except in the direst of emergencies, we will not tap this reserve as we build it to our ultimate goal of* [specify amount].

Try to be as specific with your other goals as well, for your goal statements will serve as financial checkpoints in the months ahead. Review them often, stay focused, update and revise as priorities change, and be diligent in applying your newfound financial wisdom. You'll be pleasantly surprised at how the path to financial freedom becomes clearer as you go, as you cruise right past all those side trails to Goosechase Gulch.

LESSON OF THE DAY

Clear financial goals are checkpoints along the path to financial freedom. I will develop my Top 5 goals within the next two weeks, then review and update my goals often.

"If the Shoe Fits, Charge It"

Consumer debt doesn't get you ahead; it holds you back

Sara: "What would you do if you had all the money in the world?"

Sam: "I'd apply it to my debts as far as it would go."

Do you feel like Sam? That your debts are mounting faster than your ability to pay them? That you could do so many positive things, give more, save for retirement, and feel financially free if only you could get out of debt?

Credit can be a tremendous asset to individuals and families who respect it for what it is: a tool to help them acquire appreciating assets such as a home, investment real estate, a promising business, or other select assets.

The reality of our society is that good credit is necessary for much of the routine business of life. Lenders want to see a positive credit history before they loan us money for our new home, automobile, college education, or business venture. A valid credit card is almost mandatory for renting a car or staying in a hotel. And, while many business establishments now use computerized check validation systems, there are still those requiring a credit card as supplementary I.D.

Like most good things in life, credit is meant to be used wisely, not abused. Where many of us get into some trouble is in the use of *consumer credit*: those charge cards, credit cards, loans-by-mail, and even some home equity loans used for perishable or depreciating items. I remember a young couple who talked with me following a financial planning seminar. Married just seven months, they had accumulated debts of more than $17,000 on several credit cards for furniture, clothing, and appliances. Interest rates for these purchases averaged more than 19 percent annually, obligating them to approximately $3200 per year in interest payments alone. With monthly take-home pay of $2200 and minimum monthly credit card payments totaling $1200, they were hard-pressed to pay their rent, purchase food, and provide for the other necessities of life. Savings and investment, of course, were out of the picture entirely.

The average American family holds a credit card debt of nearly $7000 on seven to eight cards. Keep in mind that if this is the *average,* untold multitudes carry consumer debt far above that amount. And this does not include notes owed on cars, trucks, sports utility vehicles, or expensive toys such as RVs, campers, or most all-terrain vehicles.

THE DILEMMA OF STUFF

Consumer credit, and the ease with which we can attain and use it, has created a dilemma:

1. We want to look and feel financially successful, so we want the Stuff we think financially successful people should have. Saving for it is out of the question; it takes too long, and we

want to look and feel financially successful *now.* So we simply say "Charge It" so we can take our Stuff home today.

2. But a funny thing happens as we accumulate the Stuff we think will help us feel good: We find ourselves in a quagmire of debt. The Stuff that was such a "must buy" isn't nearly as fun or interesting several weeks or months after we purchased it, and the monthly payments, with interest, continue unabated. Our "must buy" has become a "must pay." To service the debt, we must short-change our present and our future. Instead of financial freedom, we're in financial bondage. Which doesn't feel good at all.

I don't know whether you're one of those individuals or families deeply mired in consumer debt. I hope not. The harsh truth is that consumer debt does not get you ahead; it holds you back. Purveyors of credit cards won't tell you this. Neither will the department stores, or the TV shopping channels and infomercials, or all those websites for purchasing Stuff on the Internet (www.poorhouse.com). All they want you to do is buy now. They don't care how long it takes you to pay off your card debt—the longer, the better.

BEWARE THE PITCH

Credit card companies virtually beg us to sign up for high credit limits and immediate cash advances of thousand of dollars. If your mailperson is like mine, almost every week she brings you a friendly letter from a bank president in Anywhere, USA, which begins something like this:

Dear Mr. and Mrs. Smith:

Because of your outstanding credit history, you are already PREQUALIFIED to enjoy the prestige and convenience of owning your very own platinum Anywhere Bank credit card . . .

The letter, accompanied by a slick brochure picturing a carefree couple strolling along an exotic beach, goes on to extol the incredible peace of mind you'll have once that platinum credit card is in your possession. Why, this nice bank president will even send you a check for your first $2500, conveniently charged to your new card, to tide you over until your personally engraved platinum card arrives.

Just imagine the prestige and freedom you will feel now that you can afford that long-delayed dream vacation or new wardrobe. Why, you can even use your card to consolidate and pay off your other cards! And receive more cash advances whenever you want, at thousands of convenient locations around the world.

BUT WAIT! THERE'S MORE!

That's right, there are still more benefits to carrying your very own Anywhere Bank platinum credit card. Every time you charge a purchase to your card you will accumulate "points" toward a beautiful gift of your choosing. Earn enough points and you qualify for your choice of a luxurious pen and pencil set, a 7-speed blender, or a cordless nose-hair trimmer.

By now you're supposed to be so excited about all the cool things you can do with your very own platinum credit card that you'll sign right up, totally ignoring the hidden message of the mailing. What the nice bank president doesn't include in his letter (but *does* put in tiny print on the back of the handy "Make Your Dreams Come True" application form) is that he expects you to pay him back all this money he's giving you. Not only does he expect to be paid back, he is going to charge interest rates that would make a loan shark blush, then encourage you to stretch out your payments until the day the Sun City Lawn Bowlers win the Super Bowl.

Why? Because, according to *Banking 501,* that thick, complex textbook all bankers studied at the Acme School of Banking (and I quote):

> ... Such extended payments will bring in even more interest, enabling you to buy your daughter Muffy a new Mercedes for her 16th birthday.

Frankly, I would rather save all that interest so I can get my own new Mercedes or my own cordless nose-hair trimmer. But do you see how easy it is to be lured by all the offers from the Credit-Card-of-the-Month club? Most of us already have enough credit cards to fund the national debt, and financial institutions continue to blitz our mailboxes with aggressive campaigns to convince us that we need *their* card, that *theirs* is better—that we can live *now* in the manner to which we hope to become accustomed.

"LET'S JUST CHARGE IT"

Typically, we do not acquire credit cards with the intention of running them up into the stratosphere. The usual rationale for the first card or two is that "It'll be good to have for emergencies."

But then emergencies *happen.* Like the emergency dinner out. The emergency vacation. Wander through a mall with a credit card and practically any item can become an emergency. Besides, you'll pay off the full amount when the statement arrives, right?

Right. Before that moment of truth comes, another pressing need has surfaced—the VCR with 30-year advance programming from TV's shopping channel. So you send just the minimum payment to your credit card company for now. And during the next month, more emergencies become just too good to pass up. The balance grows. So does the interest. You lose, Muffy wins.

In his play, *A Doll's House,* Henrik Ibsen wrote, "There can be no freedom or beauty about a home life that depends on borrowing or debt." It's true! Ensnarement in consumer debt is one of the primary reasons people fail to achieve financial freedom. They're so busy paying for their past that they have little to set aside for their future.

Has debt bogged you down? Have you become a "servant to the lender"? Tomorrow's session will help you see where you stand, and whether it's time to take positive action.

LESSON OF THE DAY

Consumer debt doesn't get me ahead; it holds me back.

Caught in the Debt Trap?

Don't rob your future to pay for your past

Today we're going to look at your debt picture to help you determine whether you've sunk too deeply into the consumer debt trap. If you've felt even a shadow of suspicion that debt has bogged you down, that instead of controlling your bills the bills are controlling you, today's session will help reveal where you may have gotten off track.

Why is it so important to break free from the consumer debt trap? On our journey toward financial freedom, remember that the words *freedom* and *debt* are incompatible; they are contradictory, like *government intelligence*. If you owe someone money, you are obligated to pay it back, usually with interest. You are not free from that obligation until the debt is paid in full. Obligation is not freedom.

THE WAGES OF MISUSED CREDIT

On a more tangible level, today's instant gratification syndrome, combined with too-easy credit, sets us back in several ways:

1. Borrowing on depreciating or consumable items (food, TVs, tools, computers, "necessities," meals out, vacations, or anything else that does not *appreciate* in value over time) is just plain bad investment. You'll pay up to 21 percent interest—often for several years—while the item rapidly (sometimes instantly) decreases in value.

2. Servicing your debt prevents you from doing more positive things with your money, such as saving and investing for future needs and dreams.

3. Borrowing can place you at a *relational* disadvantage as well as financial. Think about it: When you're in the room with someone to whom you owe money, are you fully comfortable? The ancient proverb speaks wisely for today: "The rich rule over the poor, *and the borrower is servant to the lender*" (Proverbs 22:7, emphasis added).

WHERE DO I STAND?

Where do you stand when it comes to consumer debt? On solid ground or in the quagmire? Let's find out. Arise, and take this book with you to the place where you keep your financial records, such as your desk, kitchen, or crawlspace. Pull out your calculator and a pencil. Take a few quiet moments to honestly answer the following questions.

1. Do my/our consumer debts total more than 15 percent of annual take-home pay? Yes/No.

Get out your most recent credit and installment card statements, car payment information, and any other documents showing what you presently owe for items or expenses which have been consumed (i.e., vacation, food, gasoline) or are depreciating in value (i.e., furnishings, vehicles, clothing).

If you have taken out a home equity loan or carry a balance on a home equity line of credit, do not include expenditures you may have made from these sources to increase the basis (assessed value) of your home, such as a finished basement, a permanent addition, trees or landscaping. Such expenditures are usually not considered consumer debt because, more likely than not, they are invested in an *appreciating* asset. However, if you have made the common mistake of using a home equity loan or line of credit for a consumable or depreciating item, be sure to include the total of those expenditures in this calculation of your total consumer debt.

With all those statements stacked neatly in front of you, now comes the question: *How many trees have I killed?* We may never know the answer, but I promise you'll be more environmentally friendly in the future.

Now add all your current balances. The sum is your *total consumer debt*. Your calculator should have enough digits to display this sum.

Take your total consumer debt and divide it by your annual take-home pay. If the result is more than 15 percent, consumer debt is playing too big a role in your financial life. Ten percent is better, but still too high to experience financial peace of mind. Ideally, we want to bring your consumer debt down to zero and keep it there.

2. Do I/we consistently pay only the minimum amount due each month on installment or credit card purchases? Yes/No.

Remember, paying only the minimum amounts due is how creditors make money. Your money. It's in their best interest that you pay them as little as possible for as long as possible. They want the awesome power of compounding interest to work in their favor, not yours. Remember, Muffy's already driving her new Mercedes; she also has a very expensive college in mind. Any time you let interest accrue on consumer debt by not paying in full, you are allowing compound interest to work against you—at the profit of someone else.

3. Do I/we tend to add more expenses to a credit account than we can pay off at the end of the same month? Yes/No.

If you add $75 in charges this month and make a payment of only $50, you've carried $25 over into next month on top of your existing balance. That carryover will accrue interest, making your balance even bigger. Continue this from month to month and you have the proverbial snowball effect.

4. Do I/we find we're charging consumable or depreciating items that were formerly purchased with cash? Yes/No.

Meals out, vacations, gasoline, oil and lube services, clothing, or anything else that is consumed or that depreciates in value should be paid for with cash. Do not put such items on credit unless you have the firm resolve and discipline to pay these charges in full when the statement arrives. Most people do not, unless the sum of such purchases is very low. But why tempt yourself? Just two or three of these modest expenditures can add up.

5. Do I/we have an inner "lack of peace" about our consumer debt situation? Yes/No.

If you've been fighting that "gotta get out of debt" feeling, or have ever had to say "maybe when I get out of debt . . ." or have experienced worry over your financial obligations, you are experiencing symptoms of financial bondage instead of financial freedom. Financial freedom means freedom from worry and obligation, an inner peace of mind that results from wisely keeping your spending and consumer debt under control. If you've felt an inner lack of peace about your debt picture, it's time to get tough with yourself and take the necessary steps to turn your situation around.

6. Have I/we received any late-payment penalties, or letters or phone calls about late payments? Yes/No.

Late payments are a sure sign that you're having to juggle your finances due to excess commitments.

7. **Am I/are we unable to consistently put at least 10 percent of take-home pay toward savings? Yes/No.**

As we saw on Day 5, an automatic savings program of a minimum 10 percent of your take-home pay is a fundamental secret of financial freedom. Saving less than that is going to prevent you from reaching your goals. If servicing consumer debt forces you to cheat yourself on your savings program, your consumer debt is too high.

IF YOU ANSWERED "YES" . . .

If you answered yes to any of these questions, it's possible you have allowed the "Buy Now, Pay Forever" syndrome to mire you in debt. If so, you're making your present financial life much tougher than necessary. You're *definitely* compromising your future financial strength by using today's dollars to pay (with high interest) for things that happened weeks, months, or years ago. Perhaps most seriously, your finances may actually be in jeopardy without a swift and sure mid-course correction.

But please don't despair—this doesn't mean you're a bad person. You're a good person who simply encountered a bad streak of luck or made a bad decision or two. People in far worse shape have become debt-free, and so can you.

And it's going to feel so good.

LESSON OF THE DAY

I refuse to rob my future to pay for my past.

DAY 11

Escape the Debt Trap

From this day forward, think DEBTFREE

Yesterday you tiptoed through an important seven-question analysis to determine whether too much consumer debt has wormed its way into your financial life.

Take a moment to review your answers to those questions. If you answered yes to any of them, you're either flirting with trouble or you've already found it. But we're going to change that, beginning today!

Mark this day on your calendar: Turnaround Day. Today is the day you begin to regain control of your consumer debt picture. You're going to put a stop to the harmful habits that led you toward trouble and begin the process of becoming DEBTFREE.

Oops, did we miss a typo? Nope. Against my editor's better judgment I've deliberately combined two words into one to help you remember this important term. (I are a editor to, you no.)

Think about this concept for a moment: DEBTFREE. Imagine the incredible benefits you're going to experience when you are free of consumer debt . . .

THE JOYS OF BEING DEBTFREE

First, you're going to be in control of your cash flow. When you no longer have to service those debilitating monthly debt payments, you will have more money to enjoy life, handle emergencies, give to your church or favorite charity, build your savings reserve, and invest for future dreams.

Second, you'll stop the drain of compound interest working *against* you and get it working *for* you. Instead of paying 16, 18, 20 percent on the money you owe, you'll be earning 5 to 15 percent (sometimes more) on those funds as you redirect them toward savings and investments. Eliminate the pay-out, add the earnings, and in effect you're earning 21 to 35 percent on those dollars!

Third, you'll feel financially free. No longer will you feel like a "slave to the lender," making endless payments on depreciating or already-consumed purchases. Peace of mind is one of the best investments you'll ever make.

Fourth, you'll be able to make future purchases with cash. When there's a genuine need or you just want to do something for the fun of it, you'll pay with cash instead of plastic. With your rejuvenated savings program, the funds will be there for you, designated for just such an event. You won't spend months or years and countless interest dollars paying for your purchase. You'll be in charge instead of the lender charging you.

DEBTFREE.

It makes financial sense, and it's a wonderful place to be. Today you're going to launch a simple but powerful strategy to get there, and believe me, you'll begin enjoying the benefits almost immediately.

THE CRUCIAL STARTING POINT

How do you get out of debt? Beginning *immediately* (which, in the original Greek, means "immediately") take these first few important steps:

1. Commit yourself to no more consumer debt.

Boldly. Irrevocably. Other than your home mortgage (which in most cases is an appreciating asset) and possibly a car loan (we'll help you get control of auto expenses later in this 21 Day program), your goal is to eliminate all consumer debt and turn debt-servicing dollars toward YOU-servicing dollars—savings and investment for your future, not Muffy's. From this day forward, you're going to cease robbing your future to pay for your past. You're going to operate on a cash basis.

As you make this commitment, continue to think *DEBTFREE*. When temptation waltzes into your brain to charge something (and it will), think *DEBTFREE*. If you feel you need something now but would have to put it on credit, think *DEBTFREE*. It's your new commitment, your new way of life.

2. Reduce your card collection to One Card Only.

Just as an ex-smoker courts disaster if she keeps packs of cigarettes around the house, so you risk blowing it if you hold too many credit cards. The average couple owns seven or eight cards, often running up one to make payments on the other. Each card comes with a credit limit of a few hundred to several thousand dollars. Lurking behind each card is a financial institution dedicated to convincing you to charge everything from Nassau junkets to nose jobs. They don't care if you're dogpaddling in debt—they just want you to build as much debt as possible so they can earn heaps of interest on what they hope is a v-e-r-y s-l-o-w payback.

Multiple cards are a bad idea because you simply do not need either the motive or the means to accrue tens of thousands of dollars in consumer debt. Let's be honest: The temptation is just too great. Whether you max out one card or spread your charges among several, it's far too easy to justify excessive spending by saying, "It's okay, we have the credit."

Today, retake control of your credit by narrowing the sum total of your credit and charge cards to one. Not one *handful*, one *card*. Select the all-purpose card (MasterCard, VISA, Discover) with the lowest interest rate. This is the one (and only) card you're going to keep for check-writing identification, car rental, or a genuine stuck-out-in-the-boonies emergency. Then (are you ready for some fun?) take the other cards, every single one of them, insert between scissors, and transform those cards to confetti.

That's right, slice away. It may hurt a little—remember, it always hurts when you slice a cancerous growth from your body but you're so much healthier afterward! You're doing the smart thing—making an instant improvement in your personal finances. You are not—I repeat, *not*—going to make any more purchases on these cards, nor will you need them ever again. You're going to pay off your outstanding balances and close these accounts.

This exercise includes any department store, gas station, or chain store charge cards as well. (You thought I didn't see them, didn't you?) Those establishments once looked down their noses at all-purpose cards, requiring you to carry their own chain-brand card. Today, however, virtually all of them accept VISA, MasterCard, or Discover. You no longer need the chain-brand cards, so you may wholeheartedly include them in your slice-and-dice party.

Still feeling guilty? Experiencing withdrawal pains? Don't. This step is probably the most important one you will take to improve your financial picture. You're simplifying your financial life, reducing the temptation to add to your consumer debt, and laying the foundation for becoming DEBTFREE. So don't hold back. Laugh deliriously as you slice away at these albatrosses that have been holding you down.

3. Remove temptation from your wallet.

Okay, you're down to One Card Only. If you must keep this card in your wallet, write the term DEBTFREE on a yellow sticky and attach it to the front of your card as a reminder to stop and think before you use it.

In the likely event that you've really struggled with impulse charging, make your card more difficult to access. Keep it in your safe deposit box. Or, follow the example of some other couples who have successfully climbed out of debt: Freeze the card in a water-filled milk carton. (I kid you not.) Having to thaw out the card before a purchase will force you to pause and think whether you really "need" to put a desired item on credit. You'll be amazed how the spending urge passes after a couple of hours' cooling-off time!

Whatever it takes, commit to living strictly pay-as-you-go. Make your card difficult to get to so you'll be forced to wait and think. If you see something you want but you can't afford it today, you definitely can't afford it long-term.

4. In place of a regular credit card, use a *debit card*.

Both VISA and MasterCard issue debit cards, which look and act much the same as a credit card with one wonderful difference: If you put an expense on a debit card, it is automatically deducted from your checking account. Thus, it does not accrue interest and does not add to your consumer debt. It's just like writing a check, only you don't have to write the check or show I.D.

For example, say you've just enjoyed dinner at José Gianelli's Chinese Smorgasbord, and you don't happen to have enough cash in your wallet. You don't want to pay on credit because you're committed to living on a cash basis. But, alas, José doesn't accept personal checks. What to do? Pull out your VISA or MasterCard debit card. José accepts it just as he would a credit card. You deduct the amount from your checkbook ledger, because the bank's going to do likewise before your head hits the pillow tonight. José's happy, your tummy's happy, and you're happy because you've paid-as-you-went instead of running up a credit card debt.

If you rent cars frequently for personal use, you'll want to keep in mind that, as of press time, car rental agencies are among the few holdouts who do not accept debit cards. This may change as debit cards continue to grow in popularity, but for now the agencies don't consider debit cards sufficient proof of creditworthiness. But they are the rare exception. Just about everyone else who honors credit cards also honors the debit card. You can acquire one at your local bank.

FOR AN EXTRA MEASURE OF DISCIPLINE . . .

For added discipline, you might even want to abandon credit cards entirely and work strictly by cash, check, and debit card. Just be certain that (1) you have enough funds in checking to cover the expense; (2) it's an expense your checking account and spending plan allows for; and, most important (3) you deduct the expense from your checking ledger immediately so it doesn't surprise you when the statement arrives.

Congratulations! You've taken the first steps to climbing out of the quagmire of consumer debt. Sure, it might have hurt a little, but you did the wise thing. And I bet you're starting to feel better already. Tomorrow we'll build on this progress to help you get rid of your debt for good.

LESSON OF THE DAY

From this day forward, I will think DEBTFREE.

DAY 12

Keep Running: Escape the Debt Trap, Part 2

Follow these steps to freedom from consumer debt

Yesterday you got a good start on your debt eradication program by resolving to eliminate consumer debt Forever and Ever, Amen. You narrowed your available credit and charge cards to One Card Only, and decided how to keep that remaining card from luring you back into further debt. Then you acquired a debit card to further reduce the temptation to place more purchases on credit or perhaps replace credit or charge cards altogether.

You're off to a great start, and today we're going to keep on running. Our plan of action is designed to free you from the bondage of high-interest consumer debt and redirect those dollars into your own savings account. We're going to turn a minus into a plus. So with the cry of DEBTFREE ringing in your ears, follow these steps to freedom from consumer debt:

1. **Follow through on yesterday's assignment.** If you haven't sliced up that stack of

credit and charge cards yet, we have a technical financial planning term to describe people like you: *Tsk, tsk.* Must I send the Scissor Squad to your house? (I will, you know.) Before you read another word, review yesterday's session, put the book down, grab the wallet, excise those cards, and slash away. Do it *now.* Then rejoin the rest of the class as we eliminate the trouble those cards got you into in the first place.

2. Make a list of all your creditors . . . their phone numbers, mailing addresses, the balance owed on your account, the interest rate you're paying, the minimum required payment, and your current monthly payment.

3. Prioritize your list for payment. You're going to pick off your creditors one at a time while keeping the others happy. Look over your list and determine which creditor you'd like to pay off first, second, third, and so on. You have three options here. You may wish to pay off the smallest debts first, in order to give yourself an invigorating sense of accomplishment as you cross some of those obligations off your list. Or you may wish to prioritize your creditors from "most urgent" to "least urgent"—perhaps you've received a few nasty phone calls or letters from creditors you've been slow in paying, and you'd like to rebuild your honor with them by repaying them more aggressively than the others. Another option is to rank your creditors from the "most costly" to the "least costly" by analyzing which are costing you the most in monthly interest and eliminating the most expensive debts first.

Though good arguments can be made for all three, I've found that people-in-debt seem to do best when they target their smallest balances first. Paying off a creditor and crossing him off the list provides a big psychological boost, which makes a person even more determined to continue the process. You, too, may find that the quicker you can cross some debts off your list as *Paid in Full,* no matter how small they were, the more momentum and motivation you'll gain to continue until DEBTFREEdom.

When you've made your decisions, take a separate sheet of paper and re-list your creditors according to payment priority.

4. Sell something. As we saw on Day 4, selling something you no longer need is a quick and easy way to find money you didn't realize you had. Now's an excellent time to put that tip to work. Review Day 4's suggestions of things you might be able to put up for sale through either a classified ad or a garage sale. You'll be surprised how many dollars you may raise in a short period of time.

This Found Money goes to two very important places. *Pay Yourself First* by taking half of it and sending it to your money market fund. Do it the same day you receive the money! This will help build your savings reserve so if a need, emergency, or worthwhile spending opportunity comes along, you'll be able to stay with your commitment to use cash instead of credit. Then, apply the remaining half of your Found Money to reducing or paying off the top priorities on your creditor list. You'll find that this jump-starts your debt elimination program and frees up more money to pay your other debts faster.

Temptation Alert! When you receive cash from selling Stuff or services, what's the first thing you'll want to do with it? If you're normal (i.e., if you have a pulse), you may want to devote such income to your "Hey-I've-Got-Some-Extra-Money-I-Owe-It-to-Myself-to-Go-Spend-Part-or-All-of-It" fund. How will you respond to this temptation? Right: Think DEBTFREE. When your debt is gone, then you'll have some *real* fun with the money. Until then, half of all Found Money goes to savings, half to debt elimination.

5. Assign a monthly payment amount to each creditor. Start with the minimum payment allowed. But you're not going to pay each creditor the minimum. The top priority on your list is going to receive his minimum payment *plus* an additional sum each month until he's paid up. Even if you do not bring in any extra cash, *always send at least $25 over and above the minimum payment to your top-priority creditor.* Send more if you can.

If You're Already in Over Your Head

It's possible that you find yourself so mired in debt that you haven't been able to meet even the minimum monthly obligations. If you've recently skipped payments, been penalized for paying late, or had creditors teepeeing your house, *run—don't walk*—to seek help from a nonprofit credit counseling service. For example, Consumer Credit Counseling Service (1-800-388-2227) has more than 1200 offices throughout the country. Their services are free or minimal cost, and they'll work with you and your creditors on a payback schedule you can handle. (Caution: Think twice before using *for-profit* credit counselors; after paying their fee you could be in a deeper hole than before.)

After you sell something, you may find that you can eliminate your top two or three debts entirely. If so, do it! At the very least, your Found Money can help you make a significant dent in your top priority. The idea is to make the minimum payment, on time, to every other creditor on your list while you religiously send as much as possible to your top priority. Pay him up, cross him off, do the Dance of Joy, then zero in on the next priority.

6. Make each monthly payment faithfully, on time. Never allow a payment to be late, and never, ever, make a creditor call you. No matter how deep the hole, you will climb out of it responsibly and with integrity. You'll demonstrate good faith, and feel much better about yourself, when you're diligent with every payment.

7. Once each account is paid off, formally close the account. Except for your One Card Only, you've already slashed the cards for all your credit and charge card accounts. Now, once you've paid off an account, your next joyous act is to formally close the account so neither you nor anyone else can use it ever again. There's only one sure way to do this: *Write* the company requesting that (1) they close your account, and (2) they confirm *in writing* that they have done so *at your request.* Do not let them off the hook until you receive their written confirmation, which you will keep on file as verification that the account is closed and that it was closed at your behest, not theirs.

Now comes the really fun part. Remember how we want to turn debt-servicing dollars into dollars that service YOU? Your debt elimination program is going to do just that. Every time you pay off a creditor, you're going to reward yourself by increasing the monthly amount you pay your savings program. It works like this:

8. As each debt is eliminated, designate a portion of that monthly payment to increased savings and a portion to increasing the monthly payment to the next creditor on your priority list. Read that again; it's not as complicated as it sounds. In fact, it's downright effervescing because it enables you to grow assets at the same time you're slashing liability. (If you get too effervesced, take two Rolaids and call me in the morning.)

A good starting point might be 20–80. As a debt is eliminated, take 20 percent of that monthly payment and add it to the amount you're already sending to savings every month. Then take 80 percent and add it to the minimum monthly payment you've been making to the next creditor on your list.

For example, let's pretend you've been making payments of $100 per month to Creditor #1, Wally's Wig World. Finally, the blessed day arrives when you send Wally the final payment—you're paid in full!

The first thing you do, of course, is write Wally and tell him to close your account and verify in writing that he has done so at your request. (I'm assuming you've behaved yourself and, in full compliance to yesterday's lesson, already sliced up your Wally's Wig World charge card.)

Now that your wigs are free and clear, next month you'll take the $100 you had been paying Wally and send $20 of it (20 percent) to your money market fund, in addition to whatever else you're contributing to savings each month. You'll continue doing this each month from now on. You've just increased your monthly savings contribution by $20, or an additional $240 per year.

The remaining $80 from your monthly Wig World payment now shifts to Creditor #2, the official Miss Piggy Fan Club MasterCard. This debt is now your top priority. You're going to add that $80 to the minimum monthly payment you had been paying MasterCard. If your minimum monthly payment was $30, your new monthly payment will be $30 + $80, or $110. Keep paying this amount (more if you receive extra cash during the month) until you've paid this account off as well. You then cross Miss Piggy off your list, shift 20 percent of that $110 to your monthly savings program, and add the remaining amount each month to what you've been paying Creditor #3. And so on, and so on, until you reach DEBTFREEland.

When that magic moment arrives, the birds will sing. A rainbow will span your financial horizon. You'll have eliminated your debt and increased your savings. All those hard-earned dollars you were sending to Muffy's Mercedes fund are now flowing into your savings program. You've converted the money pit of consumer debt into a positive asset-builder for future needs and dreams.

And you ain't seen nothing yet.

LESSON OF THE DAY

I will convert my consumer debt into contingency and long-term savings.

DAY 13

Now, Stay DebtFree

Keep consumer debt out of your life—for good

As you flee the muck of consumer debt, you can count on temptation to try to pull you back in. Even after you've paid your creditors off for good, you may catch yourself devising some of the best-sounding rationalizations:

- "It's on sale! It's too good a deal to pass up."
- "We've been good—we owe ourselves a treat."
- "I just couldn't resist."
- "We need to use the card to make sure they don't cut us off."
- "We'll pay the bill with our tax refund."
- "God told me to buy it."
- "Satan made me buy it."
- "Now that we're almost debt-free we can splurge a little."
- "The Lord's coming soon, so debt won't matter."
- "Just this once. We'll pay it off this month. Or next."

If you find yourself thinking this way, or perhaps more creatively, let me assure you that you're perfectly human. We're all good at rationalization; it's one of the psyche's key defense mechanisms. However, keep in mind that rationalization is what sucked you down the slippery slope of consumer debt in the first place. Maybe not all at once. But one purchase led to another, and another, until you found yourself stuck in the sludge.

You've worked so diligently at eliminating debt that I won't let you give in to temptation now. Stay focused on your goal of zero consumer debt. Once you achieve that glorious goal, what then? *Staying* DebtFree is what today's session is about.

BEWARE: MORE CONVENIENT WAYS TO GET INTO TROUBLE

I predict that you will continue to receive warm, fuzzy letters from bank presidents. You'll see tempting signs as you enter department stores: *Apply Now for Instant Credit and Receive 10% Off Today's Purchases!* And, as you draw closer to paying off a balance, the credit card companies will inform you that because you're such a stellar customer, they're going to do you a big favor and increase your credit limit. (Aren't they wonderful?)

Yea, verily, our modern financial world offers more and more easy ways to get yourself seriously sucked back into debt. They include (but are not limited to):

- An unsolicited supply of blank checks in your mailbox, courtesy of your credit card company, with your name and address already imprinted. The pitch is that you can avoid the hassle of using a credit card by simply making these checks payable to your favorite store, or even to yourself for a quick infusion of cash. The amount will be added to the balance due on your credit card. (What is not clear, unless you have a magnifying glass to read it, is that interest accrues from the moment your check is posted; there is no grace period, even if your account is paid in full.) It's a bad deal all around: Your benevolent credit card company has placed temptation in your hands, with an interest arrangement that tilts the deal even more in Muffy's favor. They have also put you at considerable security risk, for anyone could tear open the envelope and use those checks. Don't fall for convenient-checks-in-the-mail: Tear them up as soon as you receive them. Then write the credit card company and instruct them to remove your name from their pitch list.

- A credit card backed by the equity in your home. In other words, a home equity line of credit with a credit card to make impulse spending more convenient. Again, don't do it. A home equity line should be used carefully, cautiously—and only for appreciating assets such as home improvement. You should never use credit, especially credit backed by your home, for consumable or depreciating items. It's just plain poor stewardship. And if you get in too deep and are unable to pay, you could lose your house.

- TV shopping channels and infomercials. They've hired professional persuaders whose sole purpose is to convince you that you must *Call Now!* Did you notice that they don't take checks? Need I say more?

Bottom line: If you can't afford to pay cash today, you can't afford to pay with interest tomorrow. Remember, freedom and debt are a contradiction They just don't go together. You can have one or the other, but not both. Debt enslaves you; freedom liberates you. Multiple choice? Choose freedom.

TO KEEP YOUR CREDIT SPENDING UNDER CONTROL

Once you've escaped the debt trap, or if you are close to doing so, these strategies will help you keep your commitment to stay DEBTFREE.

✓ **Stick to the One-Card-Only rule**. That's all you'll need from here on. Deep six all invitations for additional cards, then write the companies and ask them to remove you from their mailing list.

✓ **Determine the maximum you will charge to your One Card Only in a given month**. With your spouse, agree on a modest monthly dollar limit you will not go beyond, no matter what "opportunities" may come your way. It should be a sum you feel you can comfortably pay *in full* upon arrival of the monthly statement without sacrificing any other areas of your budget. Need a number? Start at $30 per month, max. If you find yourself going beyond that, or not paying the statement in full at the end of each month, it's time for the scissors.

✓ **Ask yourself some tough questions**. The fact that you've determined a maximum monthly limit for credit-card spending does not *obligate* you to spend to that limit every month. So when the urge for unplanned credit card spending rears its seductive head (and it will), ask yourself some tough questions to see if this purchase is really necessary: "Why do I want this? Is it a whim I'll regret in a week? Will I want this item as badly in thirty days when the bill comes?"

Several smart people I know actually make themselves walk out of a store and return home to discuss, think about, pray, and "sleep on" an unplanned purchase before committing to it (good advice, even if you intend to pay with cash). It's amazing how much something back at the mall decreases in importance after a night's sleep.

✓ **Pay each credit card purchase in full upon arrival of the statement**. Without exception, do not allow payment of any charges to be delayed into a future month. A practical way to accomplish this objective is to actually deduct a credit-card purchase from your checking account ledger on the same day you incur the obligation. Make a clear note to yourself regarding the purchase, *circle it*, then deduct the amount of the purchase from your checking account total. When the credit card statement arrives, the total of your circled items should be the same as the total of credit-card charges for the month. Since the funds have already been deducted from your checking account ledger, you're able to write a check to the credit card company, paying your new balance in full.

✓ **Avoid future debt burdens and finance charges by saving in advance for major purchases**. Disciplined debt management enables you to be much more aggressive in your savings program. And by saving in advance for future needs, you can help prevent future debt obligations and costly finance charges. So if you haven't already done so, now's the time to begin setting funds aside for all those wonderful things the nice bank president wanted you to charge to your very own platinum credit card. From now on, you're going to pay cash, from checking or savings, for all depreciating or consumable items.

✓ **If you find you're still running up your One Card Only, shift to a debit card**. If the sticky note, safe deposit box, or freezer doesn't cure you of credit card codependency, your course is clear: Take the offending credit card and give it the scissor treatment. You don't need that source of credit; it's doing you more harm than good. Slash it up, pay it off, close it down. From now on, let your debit card be your means of payment when you can't write a check or pay cash. Properly used, it will help impose the discipline you need to stay current.

✓ **And finally** ... Of course, we can't conclude our debt-nuking days without repeating the key to keeping consumer credit under control. All together now: *Think DEBT-FREE.* As we've emphasized, this is one of the most crucial commitments you will make as you journey toward financial freedom.

IT'S WORTH THE EFFORT!

During the past five days we've seen how to escape, and stay clear of, the debt trap. Worth the effort? You bet. Can you do it? Absolutely. Should you? Hey, we're talking financial freedom here.

When you keep consumer debt under control, you'll feel a greater sense of security, control, and peace of mind. You won't feel so "strapped" between paychecks; your monthly cash flow will be enhanced. You will have more discretionary dollars the following month, enabling you to purchase with cash instead of expensive credit. You will build a savings reserve to cover true emergencies and to pay-as-you-go on vacations or other major purchases. You'll be able to invest more diligently for the long term so you'll be financially independent when retirement comes—free from dependence on your children. Most important, as you better provide for your family and your future, you'll also be able to give more to your church, to a worthy charity, or to someone in need.

And we're not just thinking "years down the road." Blast away at debt, stay true to your resolve, and you'll begin reaping the rewards right away. You will truly understand what we mean when we emphasize: *Get rid of consumer debt—for good.*

LESSON OF THE DAY

I will keep consumer debt out of my life—for good.

DAY 14

Turbocharge Your Long-Term Savings

Uncle Sam actually wants to help you save. Is he feeling all right?

What would you think if I told you of a savings vehicle in which you'll receive an immediate 15 to 28 percent cash return on your money—*and* the likelihood of earning an average of at least 10 to 15 percent annually?

No, I'm not asking you to speculate in pork bellies. The savings vehicle that offers these results comes to you courtesy of that feisty uncle of ours: Uncle Sam. That's right, the same Uncle I called "greedy" earlier. (I felt ashamed for saying that, but I got over it.)

What happened was that one day Uncle Sam wasn't feeling quite like himself, and an amazing thing happened. In a rare admission that maybe government can't provide everything to everyone after all, he established a set of programs to actually encourage individuals and families to save part of their earnings for the retirement years. What a concept! Bless his heart, and all his other vital organs, he even provided incentives by making some contributions *tax-deductible* and all earnings *tax-deferred*, which can trim hundreds of dollars off each year's tax bill and help our savings compound much more dramatically.

It's hard to figure Uncle Sam: a bully one day, benevolent the next. Regardless of what brought on his temporary sanity, it's now law and it's to our advantage. In fact, these long-term savings strategies are so powerful that, if you're not already doing so, you'll want to put one or more of them to work as soon as possible.

THE 401(K)

The 401(k), creatively named after the section of the tax code that defines such things, is designed for employees of for-profit companies. If you are said employee and your company offers said benefit (I'm studying government-speak in case I run for Congress), I urge you to jump on the 401(k) the moment you qualify. Some employers require a one-year waiting period for new employees; others let you start right away.

Here's how it works: You instruct your employer to automatically deduct up to 15 percent of your gross salary from your paycheck. (There is a specific per-year dollar limit, which changes periodically, so ask about the current limit.) Each contribution is invested per your direction in one or more of a selection of mutual funds. Usually you will have at least three funds to choose from; most plans offer five or more including a growth stock fund, a more conservative stock fund, a bond fund, a blended fund (stocks and bonds), and a money market fund.

Part of the beauty of the 401(k) is that you are Paying Yourself First, automatically, before you even see your paycheck. It's one of the most disciplined, painless ways available to make sure you save for your long-term future. But it gets better:

- Contributions to a 401(k) do not count as reportable income in the year you make them; they are free from federal and state taxes. Thus, depending on your tax bracket, you virtually earn an immediate 15 to 28 percent cash return on your contributions—taxes you don't have to pay. You *will* pay the going income tax rate as you withdraw these funds later in life, and there are penalties for withdrawal prior to age 59½, but the 401(k)'s advantages far outweigh the restrictions.

- By investing in stock mutual funds, you're investing in vehicles that historically have averaged better than 10 percent annually. In recent years many stock funds have done far better than that.

- Your investments can be as conservative or aggressive as your tolerance for risk.

- Many employers, though not required to do so, offer programs in which they "match" your contribution to your 401(k) up to a maximum of 5 to 6 percent of your salary. While you maintain investment control of employer matches, they usually are on a vesting schedule, which means that should you leave the company after one year in the plan you qualify to take 20 percent of employer contributions with you; after two years, 40 percent, and so on until you are 100 percent vested.

- You can diversify your investment among different types of mutual funds for added safety.

- Your earnings are tax-deferred until withdrawal, when they are taxed as ordinary income. By not having to pay taxes on earnings each year, your retirement savings can compound more powerfully.

- While the 401(k) penalizes for early withdrawals, you are allowed to take out a loan from your account. You must pay yourself back with interest, but the principal and interest go to your account—you virtually are your own banker. Keep in mind, however, that any time you dip into retirement savings you've set yourself back and will have to scramble faster later on to rebuild what you need. So I don't recommend tapping retirement funds early except under dire circumstances. (Vacation to Tahiti: nice but not dire.)

As with any investment, past performance of a mutual fund is never a guarantee of future results. Sometimes the stock and bond markets are more emotional than logical; they'll go up if the Fed chairman sees his shadow and down if he doesn't. But generally speaking, a well-managed stock mutual fund will ride out the ups and downs over the long haul, and with a 401(k) or other retirement plan, you're definitely in it for the long haul.

THE 403(B)

This is 401(k)'s cousin, also named for a section of the tax code. It comes right after section 403(a), "Demographic Delineation of Doughnuts Devoured by Democratic Donors." The 403(b) is available to employees of nonprofit organizations such as schools, hospitals, ministries, and charitable or service organizations. 403(b)s allow contributions of up to 20 percent of gross salary (with annual limits subject to change), and contributions are federal and state tax-deductible. You may know the 403(b) as a *tax-sheltered annuity (TSA)* because it typically includes insurance-related products, but don't hold that against it. It's a solid retirement savings program with benefits similar to the 401(k). If you work for a nonprofit organization, take advantage of this opportunity as soon as you qualify.

INDIVIDUAL RETIREMENT ACCOUNTS

While Individual Retirement Accounts (IRAs) have been around a while, the Taxpayer Relief Act of 1997 has added a few tweaks, mostly good. IRAs now come in several flavors:

Traditional IRA

Any wage earner, whether he has a company-sponsored retirement plan or not, can open and contribute up to $2000 each year to a traditional IRA. Contributions to this IRA are tax deductible if you do not have a retirement plan at work; they are partially tax deductible if your annual adjusted gross income is under specified limits. If you do have a company-sponsored retirement plan, you can still contribute to an IRA on a nondeductible basis. However, you'll want to max out your company plan first to take full advantage of tax deductibility and matching programs.

IRAs can be set up through banks, insurance companies, brokerage firms, and mutual fund families. Ignore the first three because of axes to grind, limited financial products, and probable sales commissions; set up your IRA through a reputable no-load (no-sales-commission) mutual fund family such as Vanguard, Fidelity, or American Century. Most will even put you on an automatic monthly draft if you request it, giving you the Pay Yourself First advantage.

Spousal IRA

For the "nonworking" spouse, this IRA traditionally has allowed tax-deductible contributions of up to $250 per year. Thanks to 1997's tax tweaks, the limit is now increased to $2000. As long as one spouse has no earned income or is not covered by a company plan, couples with adjusted gross income up to $150,000 may contribute to a spousal IRA on a fully tax-deductible basis. As with other IRAs, taxes are deferred on earnings.

You can begin to see the power of combining one or more programs as your cash flow allows: Let's pretend that Patrick has a 401(k) program in which his company matches up to 5 percent of his salary. His wife, Marie, is a stay-at-home mom. This couple can (1) contribute 15 percent of Patrick's salary to his 401(k) and receive matching benefits, and (2) contribute

$2000 to Marie's spousal IRA—all on a tax-deductible basis and tapping the compounding power of tax deferral on all earnings. After taking advantage of these tax-deductible options, they may want to contribute to traditional IRAs as well, though those contributions would be non-deductible.

The Roth IRA

Also effective tax year 1998 is the new Roth IRA, named after the senator who headed the Senate Finance Committee at the time, Senator IRA. Couples with adjusted gross incomes up to $150,000 and singles with AGIs up to $90,000 can contribute $2000 per person regardless of company retirement plans. With the Roth IRA, your contributions are not deductible; however, instead of deferring taxes on investment earnings, the Roth IRA eliminates them completely. What you miss on the front end, you supposedly make up on the back end by compounding earnings over time and never having to pay taxes on those earnings. This IRA may be worth a look from younger savers who have a longer window to build tax-free earnings on investment, from those who receive maximum benefit from company plans, and those whose tax bracket isn't likely to drop after retirement. However, because the Roth IRA is so new and complex it may behoove you, even if you don't normally wear hooves, to let some time pass before jumping on this bandwagon. At the very least, invest 45 minutes with your CPA or financial advisor to analyze whether the Roth IRA is your best option.

A SIDE BENEFIT OF IRAS

Although IRAs continue to impose hefty penalties for early withdrawal before age 59½, the 1997 legislation has loosened the restrictions a bit for two common needs in today's families: college and purchasing a first home. All traditional, spousal, and Roth IRAs now allow you to make penalty-free withdrawals for college or up to $10,000 for a down payment on your first home. Unless you're young and have many years to rebuild your retirement savings, you should generally avoid raiding these important savings dollars. You don't "pay them back" as you would a loan from a 401(k), so withdrawals even for these "good" purposes will leave a significant dent.

There is also a new "Education IRA" in which you can contribute up to $500 annually on a nondeductible basis; however, until further clarification it's likely this vehicle will negate eligibility for financial aid or the $1500 Hope tax credit. Avoid this one until Congress adds another forest to the tax code to make this clear.

PROGRAMS FOR SMALL BUSINESSES AND THE SELF-EMPLOYED

The SEP-IRA

This stands for Simplified Employee Pension and is designed for small businesses or people who work for themselves. With a SEP-IRA you can contribute up to 13.04 percent of self-employment income, after deductions, up to $24,500 per year. If you have employees, you must contribute the same percentage of their pay to their accounts as the percentage of your pay you contribute for yourself. Contributions are tax-deductible, investment choices are similar to those of 401(k)s and IRAs, and earnings are tax-deferred until withdrawal.

With the dramatic increase in self-employment or small businesses-on-the-side, the SEP-IRA is worth serious consideration for anyone who earns self-employment income. As with IRAs, you can set up a SEP-IRA through no-load mutual fund companies.

The Keogh

Another, older, plan for the self-employed is the Keogh, named after a Vermont congressman who coughed uncontrollably while presenting the legislation. Depending on the Keogh program you set up (there are variations to choose from), a Keogh allows you to contribute up to 20 percent of self-employment income to a limit of $30,000 per year. Just to confirm Uncle hasn't gone entirely soft, he requires more paperwork for setting up and administering the Keogh, but it may be worth your while, especially if your potential contribution surpasses the contribution limit of a SEP-IRA. As with the other investments above, Keoghs can be set up through no-load mutual fund families.

TURBOCHARGE YOUR LONG-TERM SAVINGS

See what I mean about turbocharged savings? Yes, Uncle Sam can be nice occasionally, especially right before an election, and he has chosen to do so when it comes to retirement savings programs. In most cases you can use the Pay Yourself First Automatically principle. In many cases you can save with tax-deductible dollars. In all cases, your earnings on investment are tax-deferred (tax-free with a Roth IRA), which gives you the potential for significant compounded earnings over the long term. You can move your money between a full spectrum of mutual fund investments offering various levels of risk and reward.

I encourage you to take full advantage of these programs as you look to the long term. After just a few months, and definitely after a few years, you'll be pleased at how Uncle Sam's benevolence has boosted you along the path to a financially free retirement.

LESSON OF THE DAY

Okay, Uncle Sam has his nice days. I will turbocharge my long-term savings by maximizing tax-advantaged retirement programs.

DAY 15

A Budget You Can Live With

Try this spending plan to help attain your goals

Welcome to Day 15!

In our first two weeks together we've surveyed the Dirty Dozen—twelve reasons good people fail with their money. You've set specific goals to help avoid similar mistakes. We've addressed the importance and the how-to of giving, saving, and being DEBTFREE. You've uncovered some money you didn't realize you had and, since I haven't received your check to the "Benson to Bermuda" fund, I assume you're directing Found Money toward debt elimination and savings. And we've seen how to put booster rockets to your long-term savings by making full use of tax-advantaged retirement programs.

I realize that by now your head may be spinning. You may be wondering, *All well and good, but how do I do all those things every month? I gotta eat, ya know.* So today I want to help you pull these important disciplines together by seeing how it all might look in a given month.

I won't propose a penny-by-penny budget because we're aiming for financial freedom, not a certificate in accounting. Instead, I will recommend a basic system of percentages to overview how your monthly spending plan can simultaneously address the multiple priorities of giving, short-term and long-term saving, and debt elimination.

A BUDGET YOU CAN LIVE WITH

No one is going to give, save short-term, reduce debt, and save long-term for you; it's up to you! To help make it all happen, consider the following general budget guidelines. A and B are what your employer does for you; C is what you do once the paycheck is in your hands.

A. YOUR GROSS MONTHLY INCOME
   Less: Social Security
   Less: Tax-advantaged retirement savings such as 401(k), 403(b)
   Less: Tax-advantaged benefits such as cafeteria plans

B. YOUR TAXABLE MONTHLY INCOME
   Less: Federal, State tax withholding

C. YOUR NET MONTHLY INCOME (TAKE-HOME)
   Giving   10 percent
   Short-term savings   10 percent
   Debt Elimination   10 percent
   Living Expenses   70 percent

Keep in mind that the above plan is meant to be *flexible*. Everyone's situation and priorities are unique. You can begin conservatively or aggressively; you can select some priorities and wait on others; and you can shift percentages over time. For example, like many people, you may desire to designate more than 10 percent of your take-home pay (C) to charitable giving. I've suggested the above percentage as a *minimum starting point* for those who may not be giving regularly at all. You may instead wish to designate 10 percent of taxable income (B) or even 10 percent of gross income (A) to giving, and adjust the other percentages accordingly. "Each man should give what he has decided in his heart to give, not reluctantly or under compulsion, for God loves a cheerful giver" (2 Corinthians 9:6–7).

Another advantage of flexibility is that, as you eliminate consumer debt, you can designate those dollars to any of the other categories. You might, for example, increase giving to 15 percent of take-home pay and short-term savings to 15 percent. Or, keep these categories as-is but increase your contribution to your retirement program(s). It's your call.

FOCUS ON GOALS

The key to making this work for you is to keep your goals in mind. If you presently have no funds set aside for a major emergency such as a layoff, then building a reserve of 3 to 6 months' living expenses may be your most urgent priority. In that case, you may need to make smaller contributions to company or personal retirement programs until you've built that emergency reserve through more aggressive short-term savings. Once that need is met, you can increase your commitment to long-term savings until you're able to take full advantage of all the benefits of Uncle Sam's retirement programs. Eventually you may be able to do all of the above—or even better!

KEEP LIVING EXPENSES AT 70 PERCENT

You've probably deduced that a crucial secret to pulling all these financial freedom strategies together is that you *learn to live on 70 percent of your take-home pay*. If you cannot, something is wrong anyway, and your lifestyle needs an honest self-assessment. Maybe you have too much house for your income level, too many vehicles in your driveway, or too many Twinkies in your grocery bag. Don't worry, I'm not out to spoil your fun. Living on 70 percent of your take-home pay may appear tough at first, but I know you can make the adjustment—especially as you reduce those pesky consumer debts.

To help get your living expenses within 70 percent, let me recommend Mike Yorkey's excellent book, *21 Days to a Thrifty Lifestyle*. Mike's not one of those tightwads who wants you to make mattresses from your grass clippings. He's a regular family guy who's done some great research for you on how to save big bucks every month just by shopping smarter. Get his book and you can reduce your monthly living expenses by $200 to $800 per month. Worth a trip to the bookstore? More Found Money!

I encourage you to begin today to redirect your monthly finances as suggested above. Doing so will help ensure that you're meeting the multiple priorities of giving, saving for short-term needs, eliminating debt, and saving for long-term needs—the essential disciplines for financial freedom.

LESSON OF THE DAY

I will redirect my monthly finances toward a "budget I can live with."

DAY 16

Organize Your Financial Records

Keep your financial records organized, accessible, and up-to-date

Okay, I'll admit it. Today's exciting session could be ... well, less than exciting. I assure you it's an extremely important step on the path to financial freedom, so stay with me. We're going to get your personal and financial records in order by organizing your home financial file.

I know, I know. As exciting as TV fishing. I can't possibly match the sheer magic of watching Angler Arn exclaim, "Hey, there, Bubba, that bass sure went for your Hurricane spinner," but I'll try to keep today's session as interesting as I can. And I didn't call it an "extremely important step" without good reason.

Take John, for example. A robust man in his late thirties, John was a good husband and father, a conscientious provider, a responsible citizen. He always paid his bills on time and made sure his family's needs were met. But then the unthinkable happened. One cold, icy evening on the way home from work, John's car hit a patch of black ice and spun out of control. He died instantly when the car crashed head-on into a pickup truck coming from the opposite direction.

After the funeral, John's wife, Karen, began the painful process of settling John's financial affairs. She quickly realized that, despite their best intentions, she and John had never taken the time to organize their personal and financial papers for easy accessibility. As a result, Karen experienced the additional burden that no grieving survivor should have to bear: the added time, uncertainty, frustration, and expense of searching for needed documents.

MAKE YOUR FINANCIAL LIFE EASIER

This is why having an organized home financial file is so important. If your records are scattered between this drawer and that closet over there and a box somewhere in the basement, can you imagine how tough it will be for your spouse or other family members to sort through your affairs if you're suddenly not there?

There's another compelling reason for getting your records in order: the simple fact that you need to refer to them often. You'll be able to find documents in seconds instead of crawling around amidst dust bunnies under your bed. And when new paperwork flows into your life, as it does almost daily, you can file it within seconds instead of tossing it in a pile of "things I'll take care of someday." Being better organized will prevent much wailing and gnashing of teeth in your future.

So today we turn your financial pile into a financial file.

TIME TO GET ORGANIZED

Here's the first step: Go back to Wal-Mart. Say "howdy" to the greeter, go to the office supplies aisle, and pick up a dozen or so blank file folders and file labels.

Next stop is your neighborhood bank. Go to the customer service representative, have a seat, thumb through last November's *Outdoor Life* while she finishes her phone call, then tell her you want to rent a safe deposit box. The cost will run you $20 to $65 per year, depending on how big a box you want.

When you return home with folders, labels, and safe deposit box key in hand, grab a pen to label each folder. If you tend to write in tongues, you may want to type the labels to make your folders legible. Here's how to label each file tab:

1. Personal Information and Instructions
2. Personal Documents
3. Personal Insurance Policies
4. Property Insurance Policies
5. Household Inventory and Net Worth
6. Savings and Investment Records
7. Retirement Programs
8. Consumer Debt Records
9. Car Ownership and Repair Records
10. Real Estate Purchases and Improvements
11. Tax Returns and Documentation
12. Will and Trusts

It's okay if you do not yet have everything listed above; for example, you may not yet own a home or other real estate. But you're likely to someday, and if you maintain the file as suggested the folder will be there waiting for you when the time comes.

In several instances you'll note that I recommend keeping *copies* of certain documents in your home financial file. That's because the original documents are extremely valuable and, unless you have your own fireproof safe at home, you'll want to keep certain originals in your safe deposit box to protect them from fire or theft. It may mean two or three trips to a photocopier during the next few days, but they will be minutes and dimes well spent.

Now root through your file drawers, under your bed, and wherever else you've been piling financial records to begin gathering documents for these folders.

Folder #1: Personal Information and Instructions

This folder won't hold any documents per se; instead, you'll keep an up-to-date list here of important personal information your loved ones would need if, as insurance agents are trained to say in hushed tones, "something should happen to you."

So take out a couple pieces of paper and invest a few minutes preparing a list detailing your full legal names, dates and places of birth, Social Security numbers, military service numbers and dates of military service, date and place of marriage; names, birth dates, addresses and phone numbers of children; and names, addresses and phone numbers of former spouses and children of previous marriages.

You'll also want to list essential medical information such as the name and phone number of your doctor(s) and what each physician treats you for; and your key advisors (executor, attorney, accountant, financial planner, minister, insurance agents, golf pro) and where they can be reached.

If you have given someone power of attorney (which authorizes that person to control your assets if you become incapacitated) or named a health-care proxy (authorization to make health-care decisions on your behalf), name those people here, with phone numbers.

Write down the phone numbers for the Social Security Administration (800–772–1213) and, if you served in the military, the Veterans Administration (800–827–1000). These numbers will help your survivors process requests for Social Security and veterans death benefits.

Finally, write down the location of your safe deposit box and keys.

Folder #2: Personal Documents

Photocopies of your birth certificates, marriage certificates and divorce papers (all essential in estate settlement), adoption papers, and military discharge papers should be stored here. Keep the originals in your safe deposit box. In the spirit of government efficiency, we all need our birth certificates to prove we were born. If you do not have your birth certificate, check with your parents; if they can't prove you were born, check with the hospital and/or city government where you think you may have been born.

Folder #3: Personal Insurance Policies

Policies and payment records on life, health/medical, disability, and other personal ("people") insurance policies go in this folder, along with employer-provided policies and benefits booklets.

Since your insurance coverage and/or policies could change frequently due to job changes or prudent rate shopping, be sure you keep this folder up-to-date, clearly indicating which policies are in force and which are expired or canceled. For expired or canceled policies, mark the expiration date clearly on the front of the policies and keep them for a few years in case of a delayed claim; then discard.

Keep payment records (premium payment receipts with their canceled checks) in this file as well, attaching records to the appropriate policy. This will verify that policies were kept paid and in force.

Folder #4: Property Insurance Policies

For policies and payment records on your homeowners or renters insurance, auto insurance, umbrella liability insurance, and insurance on other properties. As with all insurance, keep these policies updated as your circumstances change. Follow the advice above for payment records and canceled or expired policies.

Folder #5: Household Inventory and Net Worth

Whether you're renting or buying your home, you should always maintain an up-to-date inventory of major furnishings, appliances, jewelry, artwork, and so forth—anything which would be costly or difficult to replace in the event of theft or fire. A copy of that inventory will go in this file; keep the original in your safe deposit box.

A household inventory can take some time to complete, but doing it conscientiously can pay huge dividends in the long run. Plus, you only have to do it once, then simply update your inventory as you acquire new items or dispose of old ones. The easiest way is to go from room to room, including your basement and garage, listing your major possessions complete with their brand names, serial numbers, purchase date, and purchase price. If you do not have receipts or warranty registrations verifying prices and dates, look for cancelled checks or credit card statements that provide this information. If you're normal, you'll have several items for which no records have been kept; estimate prices and purchase dates on these as accurately as you can.

Many people back up their inventory with photos or a home video of each item. Photographs can be especially helpful to police or insurance adjusters should you need their help. As with the original inventory list, keep photos or video cassettes in your safe deposit box.

Also in this folder, keep a copy of your current net worth statement.

Update your household inventory every time you acquire a major new possession or get rid of an old one. You'll also want to update your net worth statement at least once a year.

Folder #6: Savings and Investment Records

This folder is for documents and statements regarding the savings program you've established with a money market fund, and for any investments other than real estate or retirement plans—stocks, bonds, mutual funds, precious metals, rare coins, and so forth. You'll want to keep actual securities documents, as well as any precious metals, in your safe deposit box; buy/sell records on stocks, bonds, mutual funds, rare coins, precious metals, or other investments can go into your home file.

Buy/sell records should include the date of purchase, quantity, item, purchase price and commission paid, selling price and commission paid, and profit or loss. These records are essential at income tax time and in the thrilling event of an IRS audit.

Folder #7: Retirement Programs

Documents and statements from 401(k)s, 403(b)s, pension programs, Individual Retirement Accounts, SEP-IRAs, Roth IRAs, and Keogh plans go here.

Folder #8: Consumer Debt Records

Keep account numbers, statements, and payment records for your consumer debts (credit cards, charge cards, and financing on anything other than cars that does not appreciate in value) in this folder. Also keep copies of correspondence you've sent and received regarding your accounts—especially letters in which (1) you ask to have your account closed, and (2) the credit issuer confirms, in writing, that your account has been closed at your request. You're going to render this entire file "inactive" as soon as possible.

Folder #9: Car Ownership and Repair Records

Folder #9 is for pink slips, registration receipts, purchase agreements, warrantees, and other ownership documents for all your vehicles. It's also wise to keep copies of all service and repair records; if the repair you made just three weeks ago goes *ploooey* (terminology I learned in tech school), you can document the repair.

Folder #10: Real Estate Purchases and Improvements

When you went to the "closing" on your house, you were handed three-fourths of the world's total supply of paper and told to "just sign here." Keep photocopies of all such documents in this file, along with copies of deeds and improvement records on any rental properties, raw land, or other real estate investments. Original deeds should be kept in your safe deposit box.

Also in this folder, start a list of improvements you make to your property. Record the date, type, and cost of all improvements and file with receipts for verification. This information will be needed when you file your tax return after the house is sold.

Folder #11: Tax Returns and Documentation

A normal IRS audit (oxymoron?) can dig into your past up to three years if your friendly tax person suspects a "good faith" boo-boo; however, she has six years to challenge your return if she thinks you underreported your income by 25 percent or more. If she suspects fraud, she can hound you as far back as your previous life and as far into the future as your next one. Moral: Keep your tax records indefinitely.

Keep the last two years' returns and documentation (W–2 forms, 1099s, receipts, expense records, and so forth) in this folder for easy access throughout the year. In a storage box in your closet or basement, keep *a minimum* of four more years' tax records. Better yet, keep 'em till the Lord returns, because when he does no one on earth will be able to find you, not even the IRS, who will most likely still be here looking.

If you should lose these returns, your tax preparer or the IRS and state tax agencies can provide you with copies. However, they have copies only of the actual tax forms you filled out and not the receipts you totaled to claim your deductions. So keep the originals of receipts in a safe place, clearly labeled so they are easy to find for a given claim in a given year.

Folder #12: Wills and Trusts

Keep photocopies here, along with the name, address, and phone number of the attorney who drew up the documents. Keep in mind that laws change and your personal situation and wishes change; therefore, wills and trusts should be reviewed every few years by your attorney to make sure they are up to date.

CONGRATULATIONS!

You are now organized! Customize your folders as your financial situation changes. Eventually you may want to further classify your records by using twelve hanging files with multiple folders in each hanging file. Keep them in a file cabinet with processed mail and paid bills. Whenever you need the information, it'll be right there. More important, your home financial file will be readily accessible should something happen to you, making a difficult task much easier for your loved ones. Practically speaking, it's one of the best gifts you can leave them.

LESSON OF THE DAY

I owe it to myself and my loved ones to keep my financial records organized, accessible, and up-to-date.

Keep It in Perspective

Money is merely an implement, not life itself

We're more than two-thirds of the way through our 21-day journey, a good time to pause and catch our breath. Today, let's step back from the numbers and strategies and details just to be sure we're keeping money in proper perspective.

Throughout history, much has been written regarding the philosophy of money. Survey what men and women have written and you'll discover a full spectrum from one extreme, "God Wants You Rich (So Why Aren't You?)" to the other, "God Wants You Poor (Aren't You Ashamed of Yourself?)."

We reside on this earth only a short while. Then we move on to an eternal afterlife in which money doesn't matter. But while we're on earth, we know we're to be responsible citizens and loving, caring providers for our families. Money matters here. But how much does it matter in the bigger scheme of things?

For answers, there isn't a better source than the ultimate guidebook. While cultural mores change over time, truth by its very nature remains constant and unchanged from generation to generation. That's why the Holy Bible remains as relevant today as when it was written. And why it remains worthy of our trust. One writer aptly put it: "The Bible is God's love letter to his children." But to live by the Bible's wisdom, we need to have a pretty good idea of what it says. And it says a lot about money.

Today, let's pause to be sure we're keeping money where God wants it in our lives—in its proper perspective. Money is important, but it's only an implement to help us live life. It is not life itself. Has it become *too* important? Please sit back and read the following Scriptures carefully and thoughtfully ... and ask yourself if your finances are in harmony with God's perspective on money.

GOD OWNS IT, WE JUST MANAGE IT.

" ... for every animal of the forest is mine, and the cattle on a thousand hills" (Psalm 50:10).

"The silver is mine and the gold is mine," declares the LORD Almighty (Haggai 2:8).

BUT HE EXPECTS US TO MANAGE IT WISELY ...

Suppose one of you wants to build a tower. Will he not first sit down and estimate the cost to see if he has enough money to complete it? (Matthew 14:28)

Again, [the kingdom of heaven] will be like a man going on a journey, who called his servants and entrusted his property to them. To one he gave five talents of money, to another two talents, and to another one talent, each according to his ability. Then he went on his journey. The man who had received the five talents went at once and put his money to work and gained five more. So also, the one with the two talents gained two more. But the man who had received the one talent went off, dug a hole in the ground and hid his master's money.

After a long time the master of those servants returned and settled accounts with them. The man who had received the five talents brought the other five. "Master," he said, "you entrusted me with five talents. See, I have gained five more."

His master replied, "Well done, good and faithful servant! You have been faithful with a few things; I will put you in charge of many things. Come and share your master's happiness."

The man with the two talents also came. "Master," he said, "you entrusted me with two talents; see I have gained two more."

His master replied, "Well done, good and faithful servant! You have been faithful with a few things; I will put you in charge of many things. Come and share in your master's happiness."

Then the man who had received the one talent came. "Master," he said, "I knew that you are a hard man . . . So I was afraid and went out and hid your talent in the ground. See, here is what belongs to you."

His master replied, "You wicked, lazy servant! . . . you should have put my money on deposit with the bankers, so that when I returned I would have received it back with interest" (Matthew 25:14–27).

AND GIVE GENEROUSLY FROM WHAT HE'S PROVIDED . . .

Give and it shall be given to you. A good measure, pressed down, shaken together and running over, will be poured into your lap. For with the measure you use, it will be measured to you (Luke 6:38).

One man gives freely, yet gains even more; another withholds unduly, but comes to poverty. A generous man will prosper; he who refreshes others will himself be refreshed (Proverbs 11:24–25).

Honor the Lord from your wealth, and from the first of all your produce (Proverbs 3:9, NASB).

Remember this: Whoever sows sparingly will also reap sparingly, and whoever sows generously will also reap generously. Each man should give what he has decided in his heart to give, not reluctantly or under compulsion, for God loves a cheerful giver (2 Corinthians 9:6–7).

AND FREE OURSELVES FROM DEBT— FOR GOOD.

My son, if you have put up security for your neighbor, if you have struck hands in pledge for another, if you have been trapped by what you said, ensnared by the words of your mouth, then do this, my son, to free yourself; Go and humble yourself; press your plea with your neighbor! Allow no sleep to your eyes, no slumber to your eyelids. Free yourself, like a gazelle from the hand of the hunter, like a bird from the snare of the fowler (Proverbs 6:1–5).

The borrower is servant to the lender (Proverbs 22:7).

Do not be a man who strikes hands in pledge or puts up security for debts; if you lack the means to pay, your very bed will be snatched from under you (Proverbs 22:26–27).

Give everyone what you owe him ... Let no debt remain outstanding, except the continuing debt to love one another (Romans 13:7–8).

WE SHOULD DO OUR BEST TO PLAN AND SAVE FOR FUTURE NEEDS ...

Four things on earth are small, yet they are extremely wise: Ants are creatures of little strength, yet they store up their food in the summer (Proverbs 30:24–25).

If anyone does not provide for his relatives, and especially for his immediate family, he has denied the faith and is worse than an unbeliever (1 Timothy 5:8).

Go to the ant, you sluggard; consider its ways and be wise! It has no commander, no overseer or ruler, yet it stores its provisions in summer and gathers its food at harvest. How long will you lie there, you sluggard? When will you get up from your sleep? A little sleep, a little slumber, a little folding of the hands to rest—and poverty will come on you like a bandit and scarcity like an armed man (Proverbs 6:6–11).

"Let Pharaoh appoint commissioners over the land to take a fifth of the harvest of Egypt during the seven years of abundance.... This food should be held in reserve for the country, to be used during the seven years of famine that will come upon Egypt, so that the country may not be ruined by the famine...." The seven years of abundance in Egypt came to an end, and the seven years of famine began, just as Joseph had said (Genesis 41:34–54).

A prudent man foresees the difficulties ahead and prepares for them; the simpleton goes blindly on and suffers the consequences (Proverbs 13:16 TLB).

The wise man saves for the future, but the foolish man spends whatever he gets (Proverbs 21:20 TLB).

BUT NOT BE ANXIOUS ABOUT THE FUTURE . . .

"For I know the plans I have for you," declares the LORD, "plans to prosper you and not to harm you, plans to give you hope and a future" (Jeremiah 29:11).

So do not worry, saying "What shall we eat?" of "What shall we drink?" or What shall we wear?" For the pagans run after all these things, and your heavenly Father knows that you need them (Matthew 6:31–32).

Do not be anxious about anything, but in everything, by prayer and petition, with thanksgiving, present your requests to God. And the peace of God, which transcends all understanding, will guard your hearts and your minds in Christ Jesus (Philippians 4:6–7).

OR PREOCCUPIED WITH RICHES . . .

A good name is more desirable than great riches; to be esteemed is better than silver or gold. Rich and poor have this in common: The LORD is the Maker of them all (Proverbs 22:1–2).

Do not wear yourself out to get rich; have the wisdom to show restraint. Cast but a glance at riches, and they are gone, for they will surely sprout wings and fly off to the sky like an eagle (Proverbs 23:4–5).

Whoever loves money never has money enough; whoever loves wealth is never satisfied with his income. This too is meaningless (Ecclesiastes 5:10).

People who want to get rich fall into temptation and a trap and into many foolish and harmful desires that plunge men into ruin and destruction. For the love of money is the root of all kinds of evil (1 Timothy 6: 9–10).

Do not store up for yourselves treasures on earth, where moth and rust destroy, and where thieves break in and steal. But store up for yourselves treasures in heaven, where moth and rust do not destroy, and where thieves do not break in and steal. For where your treasure is, there your heart will be also (Matthew 6:19–21).

SO THAT WE'LL KEEP OUR TRUST AND FOCUS ON GOD.

But seek first his kingdom and his rightousness, and all these things will be given to you as well (Matthew 6:33).

Keep your lives free from the love of money and be content with what you have, because God has said, "Never will I leave you; never will I forsake you" (Hebrews 13:5).

Some people, eager for money, have wandered from the faith and pierced themselves with many griefs. But you, man of God, flee from all this and pursue righteousness, godliness, faith, love, endurance and gentleness (1 Timothy 6:10–11).

Be still, and know that I am God (Psalm 46:10).

LESSON OF THE DAY

I will keep money in its proper place.

DAY 18

Car Savvy

Buy smarter to reduce life's biggest cash drain

Financing a new car, truck, 4x, or RV is the ultimate consumer debt. Why? By definition, a consumer debt is money you've borrowed to purchase anything that does not appreciate in value. With very rare exceptions such as a classic car, vehicles depreciate extremely quickly. What *doesn't* depreciate much is the amount you borrowed to buy the car, especially after interest is sautéed into it. High price, interest, and lightning-quick depreciation are why it's not unusual to owe more on your new car after a year or two than the car is actually worth.

The primary truth to keep in mind when it comes to cars and financial freedom is that a car is *not* an investment or an appreciating asset. A car is an expense . . . a big one. A car depreciates . . . fast. And regardless of what the sexy advertisements tell us, it makes no sense to pay thousands more than necessary for a depreciating expense, and additional thousands in loan interest because we settled for too high a price in the first place. So . . . in this confusing, alluring world of shiny new cars, how can you be financially wise and still drive a good-looking, reliable automobile? Am I going to advise you to scan the classifieds for a 1981 Yugo? Let's spend today reviewing how to keep transportation costs from slurping up big bucks that could be put to smarter use. (We just may locate more Found Money.)

DO SOME HOMEWORK

To start, go to your library and spend an hour or two with *Consumer Reports Buying Guide,* which provides ratings, test results, going prices, and other vital information on both new and used cars. If you have a particular make, model, and year in mind, call your insurance company to get an idea of what your premiums would be should you acquire such a car.

BUY, DON'T LEASE

More and more dealerships offer leases to entice the huddled masses yearning to breathe that new-car smell. A lease is intriguing because the down payment is usually smaller and monthly payments are usually lower than for a car loan. However, you still need to come up with a down payment and security deposit. And there are subtle costs to a lease that, in the long run, can make leasing less attractive and more expensive. For example:

- At the end of a lease (anywhere from 24 to 60 months) you can turn the car in, but you then are without a car and will need to acquire another. Lease another and you start the clock all over again: down payment, security deposit, new-car registration, new-car insurance premiums. When you buy a car and pay it off, you own it free and clear and can drive it as long as you like—10, 15 years or more—with only upkeep to think about. Registration and insurance premiums get smaller the longer you have the car.

- Leases have mileage limits of 12,000 to 15,000 miles per year; exceed the limit and you'll pay a hearty per-mile premium for each additional mile.
- A lease can dock you for "excessive wear and tear," a term subject to the interpretation of the lease holder. Could be nothing, could be enormous.
- At the end of the lease, you can purchase the car for the "residual"—the difference between the original total lease price and what you've paid in. Quite often, especially on longer leases, the residual is significantly higher than the actual depreciated value of the car.

So while a lease can feel like a short-term cash-flow solution, its caveats can make it a poorer use of money for the big picture. In general, you'll do better if you buy instead of lease. Especially if you . . .

BUY "ALMOST NEW" INSTEAD OF NEW

Because cars depreciate so rapidly in their first two to three years, it makes a lot of sense to look for a well-maintained vehicle that's two to three years old. With a little patience you can find a make and model you like, properly maintained inside and out, and almost ding-free. Have a trustworthy mechanic give the car a thorough physical before you buy. If it checks out mechanically, you may even want to drop a few hundred more to make any windshield pits or body dings disappear.

Remember, too, that the price of registration and insurance goes down as a car gets older. By starting with an "almost new" car you'll save hundreds of dollars per year over these expenses on a brand-new car.

But a good two or three-year-old car is still a major expense of several thousand dollars. Never pay the initial asking price. Whether you buy from a private source or from a dealer, use your homework to decide in advance what your top offer will be and start significantly below that sum. Be prepared to courteously walk away if the seller stands his ground.

PAY CASH

Eric Tyson, financial counselor, syndicated columnist, and best-selling author of *Personal Finance for Dummies* (IDG Books, Worldwide, Inc.), agrees that borrowing for cars is unwise. He advises:

> You should avoid borrowing money for consumption purchases, especially for items that depreciate in value like cars.
>
> If you lack sufficient cash to buy a new car, I say "DON'T BUY A NEW CAR!" Ninety percent of the world's population can't even afford a car, let alone a new one! Buy a car that you can afford—namely, not a new one.
>
> Don't fall for the new-car-buying rationalization that says that buying a used car means lots of maintenance, repair expenses, and problems. If you do your homework and buy a good, used car, you can have the best of both worlds. A good used car costs less to buy and should cost you less to operate thanks to lower insurance costs.

And all God's people said, *Amen.*

Buy "almost new," and buy with cash.

But, you say, *what if I gotta have a car and have no cash?*

"Well," I reply, "I'm shocked—*shocked!*—that you have no cash. How much Found Money have you come across so far? And why isn't some of it in your money market fund, growing in a column titled *NEXT CAR?*"

If life's too expensive now, it will only be *more* expensive if you finance a car. Make every effort to pay cash.

IF YOU *MUST* FINANCE . . .

Okay. It's tough out there. If you absolutely, positively must borrow to purchase a car, please do so only after you promise me:

- you'll drive the hardest bargain you can;
- you'll shop aggressively (at least three sources) for the best financing;
- you'll finance for 36 months or less with a loan that has no prepayment penalty (if you can't pay up in 36 months, you can't afford the car);
- you'll continue making car payments after the loan's paid off . . . payments to *yourself.* That's right, keep 'em flowing to your money market fund, growing in the *NEXT CAR* column. Next time you gotta have a car, you can pay cash on the barrelhead;
- you'll drive the car till it dies. Own it free and clear, keep it serviced, and treat it like one of the family until it absolutely will go no farther. This is the best way to make the high cost of car ownership somewhat worthwhile. Most number-crunchers agree: *The least-expensive car is the one you already own.*

REDUCE YOUR NUMBER OF CARS

I grew up in a family of six, the youngest of four boys. Each of us enjoyed various and sundry activities requiring transportation, and it got especially interesting when all of us were of employment and dating age. However, at no time before I left for college did my parents own more than one car. We didn't know any better; we just assumed that families were fortunate to have a car. We planned and communicated and shared and, somehow, survived. We also walked to school three miles through the snow, uphill both ways, but that's another story.

My point is, do we *really* need all the cars and trucks we think we need? Are we teaching our children to assume they can have their own car as soon as they're of age, or are we helping them learn to work together as family? Does each adult really need a separate car to commute to work, or could we, with just a little more thought, do just fine with one car?

When it comes to transportation, convenience carries a hefty price tag. We're talking payments, interest, gas and oil, batteries, tires, repairs, insurance, and registration *for each car.* Plus the time and effort required to administer all of the above. Worth it? Get out your calculator and figure: How many thousands of dollars will we save in the next year if we sell one or more of our vehicles and "make do"? Over three years? Five?

INSURE WISELY

It pays to shop car insurance. Rates constantly change, and you'll find that the same coverage can differ among carriers by $200 to $500 per year.

You want to carry *liability* coverage of at least $50,000 per person and $300,000 per occurence. In our sue-happy culture, it's smart to supplement this liability coverage with a separate *excess liability (umbrella)* policy, which we'll discuss tomorrow.

To keep premium costs down, use the highest deductibles you're comfortable with on both *collision* (damage arising from collisions) and *comprehensive* (damage from other causes such as hail or vandalism). At minimum, take a $500 deductible on each; $1000 will save you more if you're building an adequate savings reserve to cover such contingencies. Consider dropping these coverages altogether as your car ages—why continue paying high premiums to cover damage when insurance companies won't pay more than the book value of your car?

Be sure you're taking advantage of good driver discounts, multiple-car discounts, multiple-policy discounts (if you insure home, auto, and excess liability with the same company), anti-theft device discounts, and safety feature discounts (airbags, anti-lock brakes). You can ask for a discount just because you're a nice person, but it probably won't help. Forget riders such as towing and car rental reimbursement; you'll do better on those as part of an AAA membership without the hassle of filing a claim.

WHEREVER YUGO, THERE YOU ARE

You can save thousands of dollars in transportation costs just by doing some homework, shopping smarter, and choosing the wiser path instead of following the crowd. A car is an expense, not an investment. Regard it accordingly and you'll want to keep that expense as low as possible.

And see, I didn't stick you with a Yugo. If you got one anyway, I take no responsibility for it.

LESSON OF THE DAY

A car is an expense, not an investment. Thus,
I will keep that expense as low as possible.

Insurance Savvy

Know what you need and what you don't

"Ouch!" Melanie's finger burned in pain. After a few seconds there was a trickle of blood. She stanched the flow, then applied some antiseptic ointment and a Band-Aid—but that spot on her finger would be tender for the next couple of days.

A traumatic injury, the paper cut. Fortunately Melanie had paper cut insurance. For just an additional $10 per month she had purchased the new paper cut rider on her health plan at work, so in the event of a paper cut 100 percent of her medical expenses would be covered. Sure enough, after just three months of claim forms and phone calls, her insurance company reimbursed 100 percent of her medical expenses: 15 cents for the Band-Aid and 50 cents for the dab of ointment. Not bad for just $120 per year, was it?

You've figured out by now that Melanie's not a real person, and as of press time no insurance companies offer paper cut riders. Even if they did, few people with the brain cells to work near paper would consider paying $120 a year to cover something as inconsequential as a paper cut. But I spin this absurd yarn to help you understand, and remember, an important point about insurance.

Insurance can be a wonderful thing, and most of us need it in one form or another. Insurance can also be a despicable thing in that millions of policies and riders and extras are sold each year to people who don't really need them. Which brings us to the foundational point of today's session: *The purpose of insurance is to help provide for you and/or your family in the event of catastrophic loss, not in the event of every little inconvenience.* To insure against the paper cuts of life is simply pouring more money into the Money Pit than you are ever going to recoup, even if you suffer a paper cut every day of the year. Better to pay for those pesky little cuts from your monthly cash flow or your contingency savings reserve, and hold insurance only for the catastrophic losses.

So to purchase insurance wisely, we need to first assess the major areas of life where a big, unexpected financial expense could turn into a significant crisis for us or our loved ones. The next step is to be sure that we neither *underinsure* (and fall drastically short of the minimum provision needed) nor *overinsure* (and waste hundreds or even thousands of premium dollars for coverage we don't really need). Yesterday we looked at ways to "shop savvy" when it comes to auto insurance. Today let's consider other key areas in which savvy coverage is needed.

LIFE INSURANCE

If you were to suddenly get yourself seriously killed, would your loved ones have enough to help handle the sudden absence of your income?

Who needs it?

The purpose of life insurance is to provide for dependents who would suffer a significant financial hardship upon the death of a provider, for as long as they reasonably expect to remain dependent. (Note: This rules out life insurance for singles with no dependents. It also eliminates feeling obligated to provide for Junior once he's of age and on his own, for then it's time to sever the financial apron strings and let him discover financial freedom for himself.) Whether you're a primary, secondary, or co-equal breadwinner, you most likely need life insurance:

- if your spouse and/or family depend on your income for everyday needs including food, clothing, transportation, and shelter;
- if they need your earnings to help eliminate debt;
- if you're planning to pay a big chunk of your children's college expenses from your income;
- if you and your spouse are counting on several years' additional income from you to provide for retirement.

How much?

It all depends on your debt load, liquid assets, number and ages of children, what you have your heart set on providing, and the number of years your children and spouse would need to compensate for the cutoff of your income. The idea is to provide a lump sum large enough for your surviving spouse to (1) invest at a moderate return, and (2) draw from those earnings as needed while leaving the principal sum untouched until later in life. There's a quick and general formula, named for Buck Private Julius Quick and General George Custer who, you probably recall, saw 67,000 righteously indignant Sioux crest the ridge at Little Big Horn, turned to one another, and agreed that they should have bought more life insurance. To this day, financial advisors use the quick and general formula recommending that you purchase a face amount equal to 5 to 10 times your gross annual salary. Another formula, whose origination is not as well-documented, suggests approximately $100,000 of face amount for every $500 in monthly expenses your spouse would need to replace. Either formula adds up to a tidy sum of several hundred thousand or more. So . . .

Consider level-premium term

Carrying the coverage needed gets easier when we remember Day 4: for the same premium or less, term insurance can buy you 5 to 10 times the face amount of "whole life" insurance. And you won't find these deals with the more heavily advertised companies. Shop through an independent broker who specializes in monitoring an array of companies for the best level-premium term policies and prices. Some good ones include Direct Insurance Services (800–622–3699), MasterQuote (800–337–5433), David T. Phillips and Co. (800–223–9610), and SelectQuote (800–343–1985). It's all done by phone—no salesman will knock at your door.

Note: You should never, ever, cancel an existing policy until you have been fully accepted by a new company with a better policy. You don't want to be caught "between insurance" or, worse, be denied new coverage after you've canceled an existing policy.

MAJOR MEDICAL INSURANCE

If your workplace offers a health plan, that's almost always the most cost-effective way to go. If you're in a situation where you need private medical insurance coverage, you'll quickly find that medical insurance is some of the costliest stuff around. Check your yellow pages for independent brokers who specialize in personal medical insurance coverage. Call a couple to discuss your needs. As you evaluate possibilities, keep the Paper

Cut Principle in mind: You want to cover catastrophic expense (hence the term *major* medical), but not every little medical possibility. Keep your premiums lower with higher deductibles and co-payments.

DISABILITY INCOME INSURANCE

Most people understand the need for life insurance to protect income, but disability insurance is a better-kept secret. It shouldn't be. In the event of a disability that keeps you from working (an occurence more common than we like to think) disability insurance will help replace the lost income.

A serious disability can surprise you as a result of a sudden accident or from a health condition such as chronic back or neck problems, arthritis, heart condition, or a shortage of chocolate in one's diet. Again adhering to the Paper Cut Principle, you don't want to insure against a slight problem that may keep you out of work a couple of days or even a couple of weeks. The purpose of this insurance is to provide income replacement in the event of a longer-term, debilitating illness or injury.

As with major medical insurance, the most cost-effective way to attain coverage is through a group plan that may be offered at your place of employment. However, many companies do not offer disability, and the self-employed are on their own as well. It's insurance I hope you will never need to use, but in the event of a long-term problem you'll be grateful you made the investment. Typically, disability income insurance will replace up to 60 percent of your gross income. Get as much payout benefit as you can qualify for.

Definition of disability

Accept only a policy that defines disability as being unable to do the work you usually do, or your "own occupation." Some policies define disability as being unable to work at all ("any occupation"), which is much too broad and, technically, frees the insurance company from obligation as soon as you're able to hold a broom.

Benefit duration

One key decision you'll need to make is the benefit duration, or the number of years you want benefits to be paid out. The longer the duration of benefit, the higher the premium. You can designate as few as two years and as many as "to age 65." Most financial planners advise a duration of two to five years since many disabling conditions clear up adequately to enable a return to work within that period of time.

Waiting period

Once you're considered disabled and unable to work, there's a minimum waiting period of 30 days before benefits start in. A waiting period is the equivalent of a deductible in car, home-owners and medical insurance; the longer the waiting period, the lower your premium. You can extend this "deductible" as your contingency savings grow enough to tide you over longer waiting periods. If you can, opt for a waiting period of 3 to 6 months for better premium value—but only if you have your contingency reserve built up to 3 to 6 months' living expenses.

Noncancelable and guaranteed renewable

Don't buy a policy that requires ongoing medical exams, because most likely they are cancelable at the insurer's discretion. Be sure yours specifies that it's noncancelable and guaranteed renewable.

Residuals and COLAs

What if your doctor advises working only half days, or three days a week as you recover? A residual benefit ensures that you're paid a partial benefit to compensate for the time you're still unable to work. Since many disabilities play out this way, a residual benefit is worth having. A cost-of-living-adjustment (COLA) will automatically keep your benefit in pace with inflation.

Try these sources for personal disability insurance plans: Direct Insurance Services (800–531–8000) and Wholesale Insurance Network (800–808–5810).

HOMEOWNERS OR RENTERS INSURANCE

If you're a homeowner with a mortgage, your lender probably requires you to have good homeowners insurance to protect "his" investment. Homeowners insurance typically wraps three types of coverage into one: *your dwelling, your personal property,* and *potential liabilities* arising from the fact that you're a property owner. As with most insurance, the higher the deductible the lower your premium, so insure against catastrophe instead of the small stuff. Maintain adequate savings in your contingency reserve to pay deductibles and small claims yourself.

Guaranteed replacement cost: Do it

Say you bought and insured your home for $130,000 five years ago but due to the rising real estate market it would cost you $175,000 to replace that house today. Now pretend that a tornado or a fire or the maurading Morgenstern kids suddenly wipe out your nice home. Wouldn't it be nice to receive $175,000 from your homeowners insurance company to rebuild, instead of the original $130,000? The way to be sure this will happen is to insist on a guaranteed replacement cost feature in your policy. It pledges to rebuild the home for the actual rebuilding cost, whatever it may be.

Personal property and liability

Personal property is all the Stuff you keep inside the house. Usually this coverage is a given percentage of the dwelling coverage. You can purchase optional riders for specific items of particular value if you like. Here's where the household inventory we mentioned on Day 16 comes in: By keeping clear, contemporary records of your key belongings, you'll be able to readily support a replacement claim in the event of a tornado, a fire, or the Morgensterns.

Liability coverage protects you if some dear soul sues you over some allegedly awful thing that happens on your property. If that McDonald's lady spills hot coffee in her lap while sitting in your driveway, she just might sue you over it (it worked once before). If one of the marauding Morgenstern kids falls on your sidewalk and chips a tooth while harrassing your dog, his parents can sue you. Homeowners liability insurance covers those and more serious possibilities. Carry coverage of at least $100,000 per occurence.

Renters insurance

If you rent a home or apartment, your landlord is responsible for dwelling coverage. However, you still need personal property and liability coverage, both readily available in the form of renters insurance. You can buy good policies from the same insurers who provide homeowners coverage.

Homeowners and renters insurance premiums vary widely for comparable coverage, so comparison-shop at least three companies. Allstate, State Farm, and GEICO are good places to start looking.

EXCESS LIABILITY (UMBRELLA) INSURANCE

We mentioned *umbrella insurance* yesterday when we discussed auto liability coverage. Excess liability insurance provides for you in case the McDonald's lady or Mr. and Mrs. Morgenstern prevail for a judgment in excess of your homeowners liability coverage. A million dollar umbrella policy costs only a couple hundred dollars per year, which is chump change for the protection it provides. Basically it covers personal judgments or settlements other than those directly related to your employment, and kicks in once your homeowners/renters or auto liability coverage has been exhausted. Another nice benefit of umbrella insurance is that the insurer will most likely provide you with rigorous legal counsel because he doesn't want to pay a judgment any more than you do.

Purchase umbrella insurance from the same insurer who covers your auto and residence. Because the premium's so reasonable, the insurers often *require* that you also carry your auto and/or homeowners or renters insurance with them. Which is actually a win-win, since they'll give multiple-car, multiple-policy discounts when you insure with them on all three.

LESSON OF THE DAY

Insurance is for protecting against financial catastrophes, not against paper cuts. I will be sure I'm neither underinsured nor overinsured.

DAY 20

A Mutual Fund Primer

Use mutual funds to enhance growth potential

We mentioned earlier that the U.S. stock market has averaged better than 10 percent earnings per year over the past several decades. Those figures are now skewed upward by the past few years in which we enjoyed a prolonged bull market of extraordinary growth. While we shouldn't expect such growth to continue indefinitely, most financial advisors continue to believe that, because of its long-term performance history, the stock market is where a good portion of one's long-term savings should be invested.

But if you're like me, you have neither the time nor the inclination to spend hours each week poring over charts and prospectuses and annual reports to select and manage a well-diversified portfolio of stocks and bonds. I don't intend to get a master's in finance and a bank of computers and spend each evening and weekend studying and maneuvering in the markets. I prefer leaving those tasks to professionals who enjoy that type of thing and are especially gifted to do a good job of it. My credo, which I recommend you emulate, is: *Do not try this at home. These men and women are trained professionals.*

Enter the *mutual fund,* Everyman's way to invest in the stock and bond markets. For an extremely small fee, you get *full-time, professional management* (research, monitoring, and timely buys and sells of securities) by qualified men and women who are schooled and trained to do their jobs well. You get *diversification* across a broad spectrum of promising companies. And all this according to your particular *investment objective.*

WHAT IS A MUTUAL FUND?

A mutual fund is an investment company in which investors (fund shareholders) pool their money with a fund manager. The manager invests the money in a selection of stocks, bonds, or other securities, buying and selling the securities according to his research into the profit potential of various industries and companies and his read on market conditions. The gain or decline in value of the securities held by the mutual fund are averaged at the end of each trading day to determine the fund's daily gain or decline per share as well as its daily price per share. If the fund manager sells a security, investors share the capital gains or losses generated by the sale; if a security owned by the mutual fund declares a dividend, investors also share the dividend.

There are basically three ways to make money in a mutual fund: (1) the investments owned by the mutual fund increase in overall value; (2) the manager sells securities at a value higher than when he bought them, generating capital gains for investors; and (3) securities owned by the fund declare dividends. Fund managers try hard to make these three things happen, because mutual funds are a highly competitive industry and the managers' jobs may depend on it. But despite degrees in finance and banks of computers, fund managers are human and market moods are unpredictable. So . . .

. . . there are also ways to *lose* money in a mutual fund. Like the individual stocks and bonds within the fund, mutual funds are not guaranteed or insured—very few worthwhile investments are. A mutual fund can lose money if (1) the investments owned by the fund decrease in overall value; and (2) the manager sells securities from the mutual fund at a value lower than when he purchased them. No fund manager actually tries to do these things unless his brain has been sucked out by aliens, in which case he's more likely to leave the mutual fund business and run for Congress.

TYPES OF MUTUAL FUNDS

Essentially there are three broad categories of mutual funds: *stock funds, bond funds, and money market funds.* That was the easy part. Because there are so many kinds of stocks and bonds, mutual funds come in more flavors than Baskin Robbins ice cream, with additional flavors invented every year. Most funds are designed and operated with the intent of meeting the following investment objectives:

Aggressive growth funds buy stock in newer or smaller companies that show good long-term growth potential, as Microsoft did when it was headquartered in Bill Gates' dorm room. Higher volatility (upward and downward swings in changing markets) and higher risk, but higher potential reward. Aggressive growth stocks are suited for (1) younger investors who have sufficient time to wait out the inevitable market ups and downs and recover from temporary losses; and (2) investors who have their other financial bases covered and can afford to devote a small slice of their portfolio to higher-risk investments in hopes of higher return.

Growth funds invest in companies that show good growth potential but are usually better established and capitalized, which mitigates somewhat the volatility and risk factors. Volatility and risk are moderate to high, depending on the fund and the market, with equivalent reward potential. Most investment advisors recommend that everyone who owns mutual funds have a portion of his or her portfolio in growth stocks to stay ahead of inflation and to average earnings of 10 percent or better. The proportion you own depends on your age: Generally speaking, you'll want more in growth when you're younger and less in growth as you approach retirement.

Growth and income funds invest in well-established companies that show potential for continued growth but also spin off income in the form of dividends. These actually did better than many aggressive growth and growth funds during the bull market of the mid-to-late '90s. Moderate volatility and risk because they invest in blue-chip-caliber companies, and moderate reward potential. You'll want to keep a significant portion of your portfolio in the growth and income genre.

Income funds invest in more convervative securities such as bonds and U. S. government-backed treasury bills. Low volatility, low-to-moderate risk, low-to-moderate reward potential. Conservative investors, such as retirees more interested in preserving capital than growth, lean heavily toward income funds.

Hybrid funds, or blended funds, combine two or more of the above in proportions commensurate with the objective of the fund. Kind of a one-stop-shopping experience to help you diversify and maintain a balance between stocks and bonds. These might be called "balanced" funds or "asset management" funds or similar monikers.

International funds invest in overseas companies to capitalize on the global economy. Some international funds span the globe; others are region-specific such as Asia, Europe, and South America. Depending on the stated objectives of a fund, it can invest in overseas companies that fit an aggressive growth, growth, or growth and income profile.

Specialty funds invest in specialized industries or markets such as gold mining, health care, banking and finance, real estate, high technology—you name it, there's probably a mutual fund for it. These are less diversified, so they carry greater risk—if the demand and price for gold suddenly drop, for example, the whole gold mining fund will drop with it.

Index funds are not actively managed by a mutual fund manager because they are computer-driven to hold the same securities followed by various market indices. An S&P 500 fund, for example, owns shares in the same 500 stocks monitored by the Standard & Poor 500 index. It's an easy way to mirror the overall performance of the stock market.

LOADS AND NO-LOAD

You purchase shares in a mutual fund either directly from the mutual fund company or through a registered investment advisor. Some funds pay the salesperson a sales commission (*load*) of anywhere between 2 and 8 percent of your investment, which comes right out of your principal. Invest $10,000 and the sales commission alone gives you an instant loss of $200 to $800. Not a good start!

The better way is to stick with *no-load* mutual funds, and there are plenty of excellent ones to choose from. These are usually purchased directly from the mutual fund company, although more and more registered investment advisors now offer them as well. Invest $10,000 and $10,000 goes to your account balance. It's still subject to market-price swings, of course, but at least you aren't gouged by a hefty sales commission.

OPERATING EXPENSES

Whether a load or a no-load, every mutual fund charges investors an annual operating expense fee to compensate the fund manager, cover expenses for operating the fund, and keep the mutual fund company in business. These fees are minuscule for what you get in return, and when you receive your monthly or quarterly statement the balance shown is your account value after management fees have been deducted.

It's very possible, however, to overpay these fees. Annual fees for international funds should not total more than 1.5 percent of your investment. Fees for domestic funds should be 1 percent or less. The consistent low-fee leader among mutual fund companies is The Vanguard Group; while the expense ratio for all U.S. funds was 1.21 percent in 1996, Vanguard's averaged 0.29 percent. (Are you thinking what I'm thinking? Found Money?)

FAMILIES OF FUNDS

Although the occasional orphan fund does exist, you'll find most mutual funds residing in a *mutual fund family*, which is simply jargon for a company that sponsors two or more types of mutual funds. Ideally, a family will offer at least one mutual fund for each type of investment objective. Many offer several for each category as well as an array of hybrids and specialty funds and money market funds. Vanguard, American Century, and Fidelity are examples of the dozens of fund families seeking your business. A family of funds enables you to diversify your portfolio within the same family and shift money from fund to fund simply by calling an 800 number. Almost all families offer automatic investment programs to help you Pay Yourself First.

TAX-ADVANTAGED AND NOT

You can have a mutual fund portfolio within your 401(k) and/or IRA to take advantage of the long-term tax advantages we discussed on Day 14. You can also have a mutual fund portfolio outside of these tax-advantaged vehicles. However, mutual fund investing outside of retirement plans should wait until you've covered the other key savings priorities: (1) building a contingency reserve of 3 to 6 months' living expenses in your money market fund, and (2) maxing out your 401(k), 403(b), IRA, and other available tax-advantaged savings/investment opportunities. Take advantage of the advantages!

PORTFOLIO ALLOCATION

What percentage of your investment should you invest in stock funds? How much in bond or money market funds? And what kind of stock or bond funds?

Opinions vary from advisor to advisor on the ideal portfolio mix, and much depends on your age, your assets-to-date, and your tolerance for risk. One moderate-conservative formula that's often suggested is that you subtract your age from 100, and the difference is the percentage of your total investment assets you should keep in stock funds. Keep the rest in bond and money market funds.

For example, take the mutual fund portfolio of Hodjymzkyah Smith (pronounced *Smith*), who has built a portfolio valued at $50,000. Smith is 40 years old. Subtract 40 from 100, and that means 60 percent of his portfolio ($30,000) should be invested in stock funds. That leaves $20,000. Smith decides to invest $15,000 (30 percent of his total portfolio) in bond funds and $5000 (10 percent) in a money market fund for safety and to take advantage of future fund-buying opportunities. As Smith grows older, according to this allocation method, he'll gradually reduce the percentage invested in stock funds and shift those dollars to bond funds.

The *kinds* of funds you choose depend on your temperament for risk. Hodjymzkyah wants to go for long-term growth, but there's a moderate-conservative streak in him that wisely keeps him from placing all his eggs in one basket. So he's divided his

$30,000 stock fund investment among three funds: an aggressive growth fund, a growth fund, and a growth-and-income fund. His $15,000 bond allocation is split between two different bond funds.

Another way Smith could go would be to choose a hybrid fund that makes those allocations for him. However, a hybrid fund would not be as responsive to the stock-to-bond shifts he wants to make as he grows older.

MUTUAL UNDERSTANDING

We could fill a whole bookshelf talking about mutual funds, but I hope I've whetted your appetite for these incredible investments. Mutual funds allow the little guy to be right up there with the big guy when it comes to participating in the markets—only at less cost, less risk, and less hassle. If you want to be in the stock and bond markets (and you should), mutual funds are the ideal way to do it.

LESSON OF THE DAY

I will use mutual funds to enhance the growth potential of my investments.

DAY 21

The End, the Beginning

Parting thoughts for fellow travelers

Congratulations, salutations, and high-fives all around—we've made it to the end of our brief journey. Over the past three weeks we've shined a light on the path to financial freedom, taken note of crucial trailmarkers and mileposts, climbed out of some pitfalls, and skirted around others. Most of the essentials are either in place or under way; we've discarded some bad habits and replaced them with good ones. Since review is a key to learning and life-change, let's glance back over the lessons of the past 20 days.

LESSONS OF THE DAYS

1. "More Money" isn't the answer to my financial problems. It's *what I do with my money* that will make all the difference.
2. The Dirty Dozen traps that tend to hold me back most are: _____, _____, and _____.
   I will break free of these for good.

3. First, I will give some away.
4. I probably have more money than I think. I will stay alert for Found Money, then use it wisely.
5. After giving, I will move to the front of the line and Pay Myself First.
6. I will Pay Myself First by setting up a regular, automatic draft to a money market fund.
7. I will manage my short-term savings wisely by Saving Specifically.
8. I will develop my Top 5 financial goals within the next two weeks, then review and update my goals often.
9. Consumer debt doesn't get me ahead; it holds me back.
10. I will no longer rob my future to pay for my past.
11. From this day forward, I will think DEBTFREE.
12. I will convert consumer debt to contingency and long-term savings.
13. I will keep consumer debt out of my life—for good.
14. I will turbocharge my long-term savings by maximizing tax-advantaged retirement savings programs.
15. I will redirect my monthly finances toward a "budget I can live with."
16. I owe it to myself and my loved ones to keep my financial records organized, accessible, and up-to-date.
17. I will keep money in its proper place.
18. A car is an expense, not an investment. Thus, I will keep that expense as low as possible.
19. Insurance is for protecting against financial catastrophes, not against paper cuts. I will be sure I'm neither under-insured nor overinsured.
20. I will use mutual funds to enhance the growth potential of my investments.

Covered a lot of ground in 20 days, didn't we? I hope you've been encouraged and motivated along the way, that I've helped you put some sound strategies to work in your financial life. As we wrap up our journey, let me leave you with some important parting thoughts.

LEAVE YOUR HOUSE IN ORDER

We emphasized the importance of maintaining clear financial records—for your own benefit but especially for the sake of your loved ones. You'll want to take the next step soon: writing your will and possibly a trust. If you've already done either of these, it may be time for a review and update.

If you die without a valid will, you die *intestate*. It's not a disease, it's a financial condition. When you die intestate your assets will be distributed according to the laws of your state . . . and only after lengthy legal wrangling (*probate*) that leaves your survivors poorer and lawyers richer. A will alleviates much of the exhausting confusion, delay, and financial burden for your loved ones. An attorney can draw up your will for $250 to $500. There is also excellent will-writing software available for around $50; among the best is *Willmaker* from Nolo Press (510–549–1976), which meets the legal requirements for residents of all 50 states and also enables you to prepare a living will or durable power of attorney for health care decisions.

It might be advantagious for you to also set up a *revocable living trust*, which can make estate settlement easier on everyone since it steers your estate clear of probate altogether. Nolo Press also offers *Trustmaker* software. It's probably a good idea to have an attorney review any wills or trusts you do yourself.

AND SPEAKING OF COMPUTER SOFTWARE . . .

During our time together I've had you do several important tasks with pen and paper. Now I have a confession to make: Most of these also can be done by computer with the help of software such as Quicken® or Microsoft Money®. I know, now I tell you. I wanted you to do the tasks immediately and not wait to buy and train up on computer software. But if you've got the basics down and enjoy computers, now may be the time to graduate to financial software. Both Quicken and Microsoft Money are good, but Quicken seems to get the consistent nod from experts for its thoroughness and ease-of-use. With it you can figure your net worth, write checks, maintain your checking and money market accounts (including all your savings categories to "save specifically"), formulate and carry out a detailed budget, generate spending reports, maintain a household inventory, track your investments, and run tax projections and amortization schedules.

STAY ON THE PATH

The principles we've shared and the commitments you've made are lifetime ones. If you had been making some of the common financial mistakes we discussed, you now know better! Step by step, one day at a time, stay on the path of financial freedom. Skirt those debt traps. Avoid the sidetrails to Goosechase Gulch. Harvest Found Money and use it wisely. Insure to provide in the event of catastrophe, but don't overinsure. Continue giving cheerfully, saving automatically, and investing for growth.

DO IT NOW

In personal finance, time is indeed money. The longer you wait, the more you'll have to hustle later on—and the more you place loved ones in unnecessary jeopardy. So I've tried to give you small steps to get you started and moving in the right direction. Take one step; the next is a bit easier. See some progress, and the next steps are easier still.

It's possible you've breezed through this book for the key points without implementing any of the strategies. Maybe you're shy, afraid, or you're just plain procrastinating till "someday." Remember that procrastination is costly. I don't know who said "A journey of a thousand miles begins with a single step" (I know it wasn't the Vermont congressman with the coughing spell), but it's so true. The best way to get something done is to begin.

KEEP MONEY IN PERSPECTIVE

Money matters. We wouldn't have taken this journey if it were not so. But money is merely an implement of life, not life itself. Never allow money to become a preoccupation or a source of anxiety. God created us for joy, but we can't be joyful if our eyes are on the money instead of the Maker.

The fact is that all the money in the world won't measure up to the richness of a happy family, good friendships, personal growth, a close walk with God, and sharing his love with others. Those are our highest callings.

As we pursue them, we are wealthy indeed.